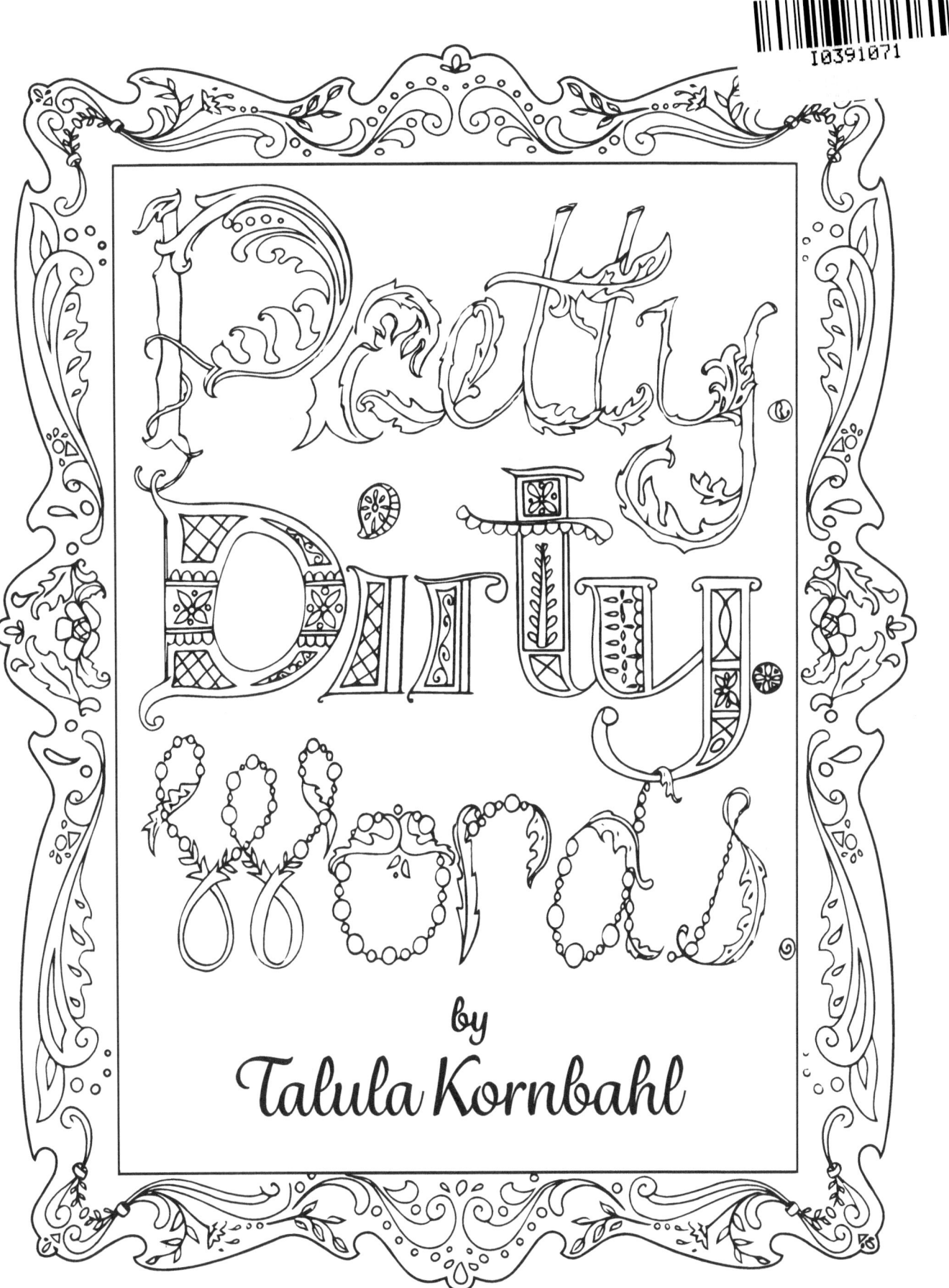

Pretty Dirty Words

by
Talula Kornbahl

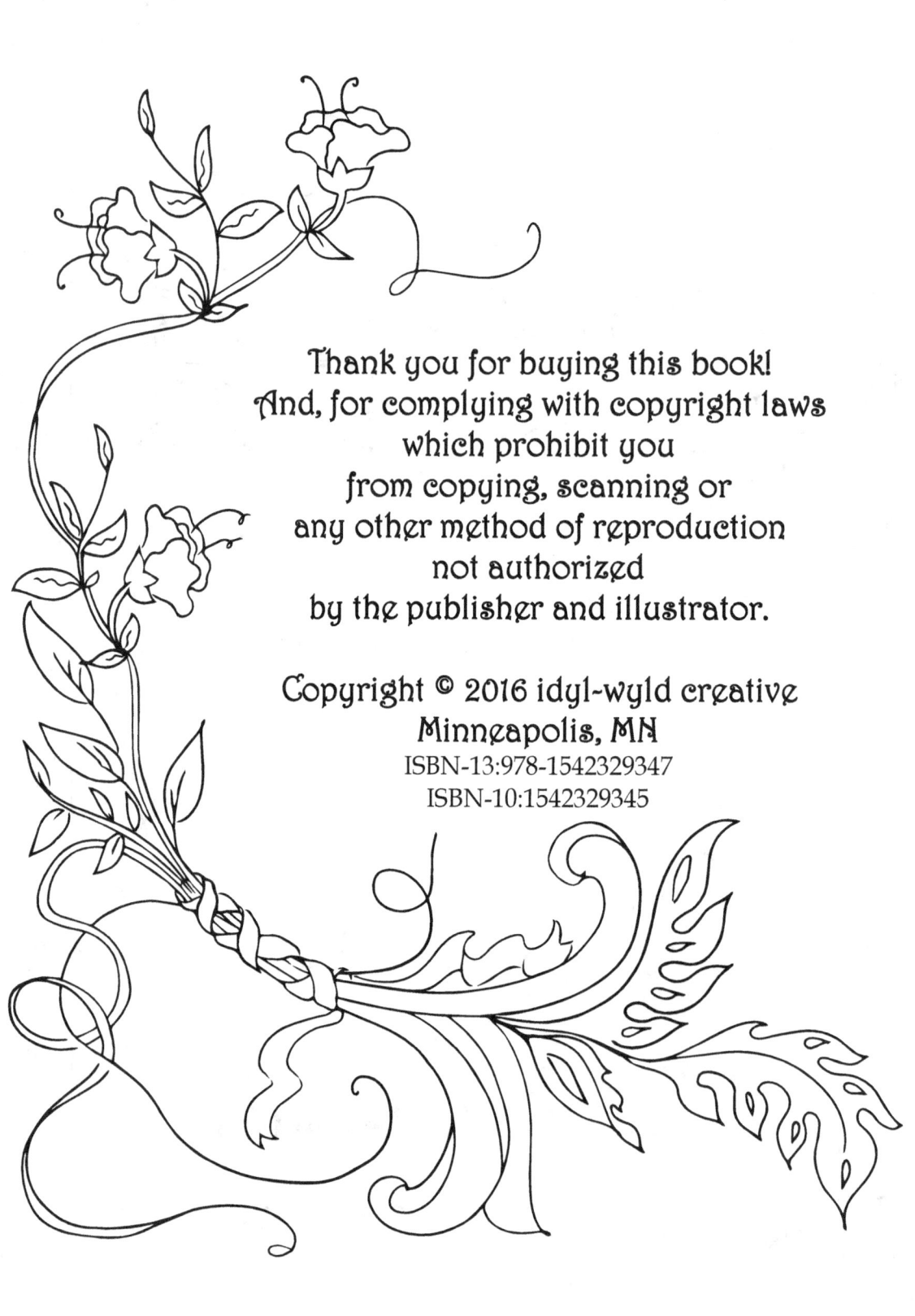

Thank you for buying this book!
And, for complying with copyright laws
which prohibit you
from copying, scanning or
any other method of reproduction
not authorized
by the publisher and illustrator.

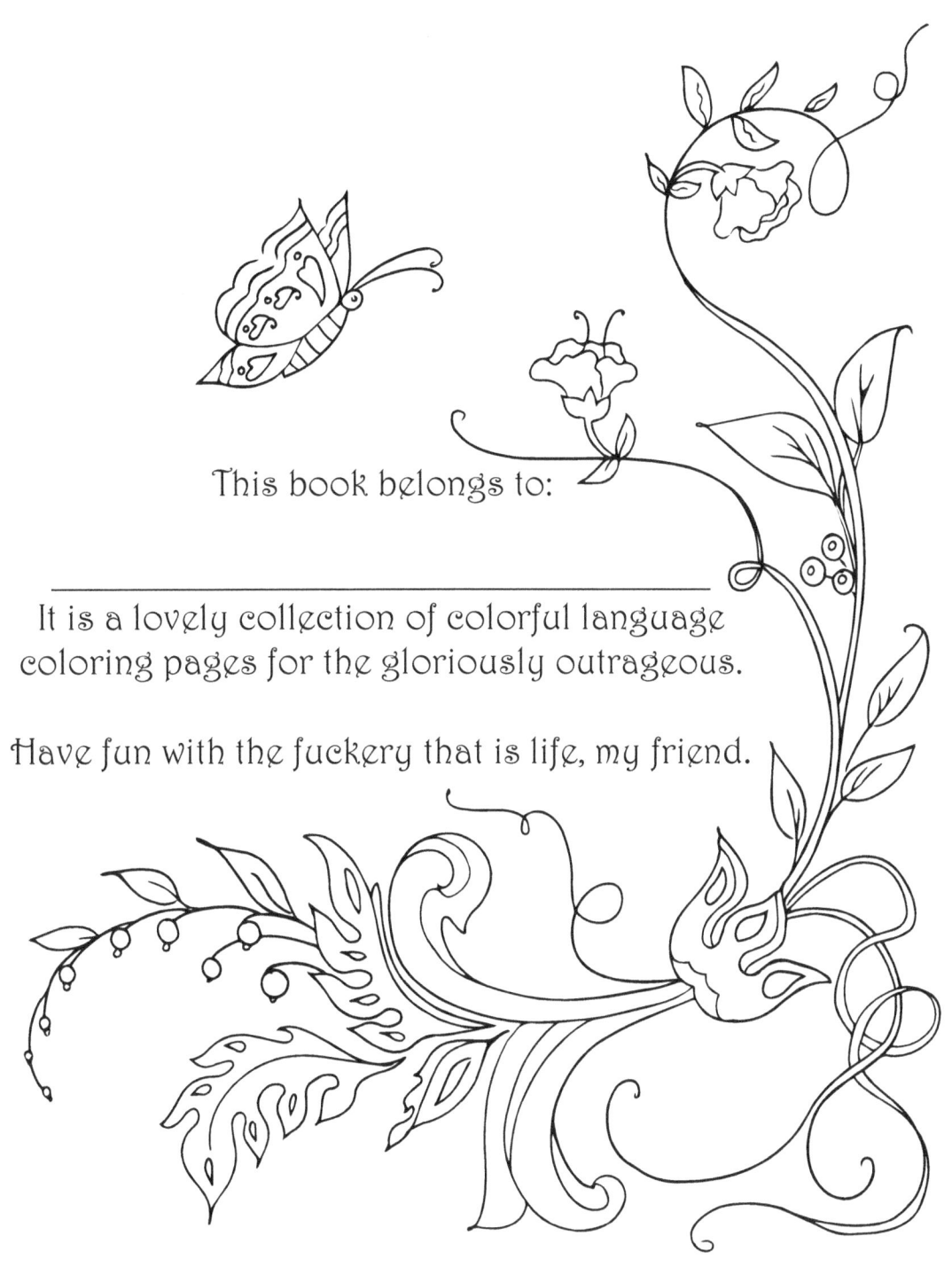

This book belongs to:

_____

It is a lovely collection of colorful language
coloring pages for the gloriously outrageous.

Have fun with the fuckery that is life, my friend.

Table of Contents

Shit
Fucks Given, Zero
Je M'em Fou
Eat Me
Arse Face
Dickhead, Prick, Douche Bag
Dumb as Fuck
Ass
Bullshit
Cock Gobbler
Cunty
Moist
'Imma Frame this Bitch
Shit Bird
Nut Less
F.U.
Bastard
Tosser
Wanker
Shit Show
Dusty Twat
Fanny Flaps
Stay Classy
Fils de Salope
Fuck it
Because rage
Piss Off

Well...

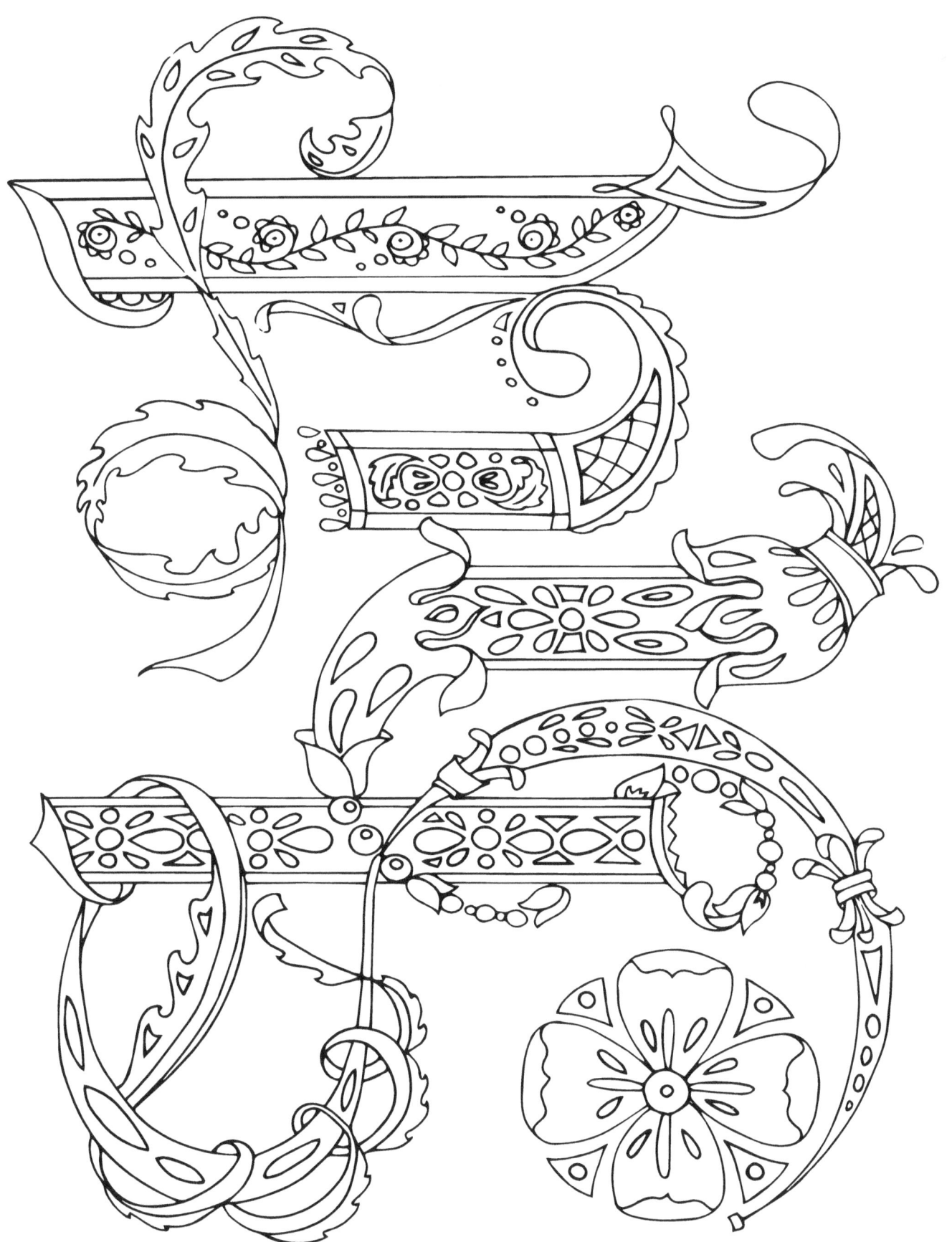

Not a one...

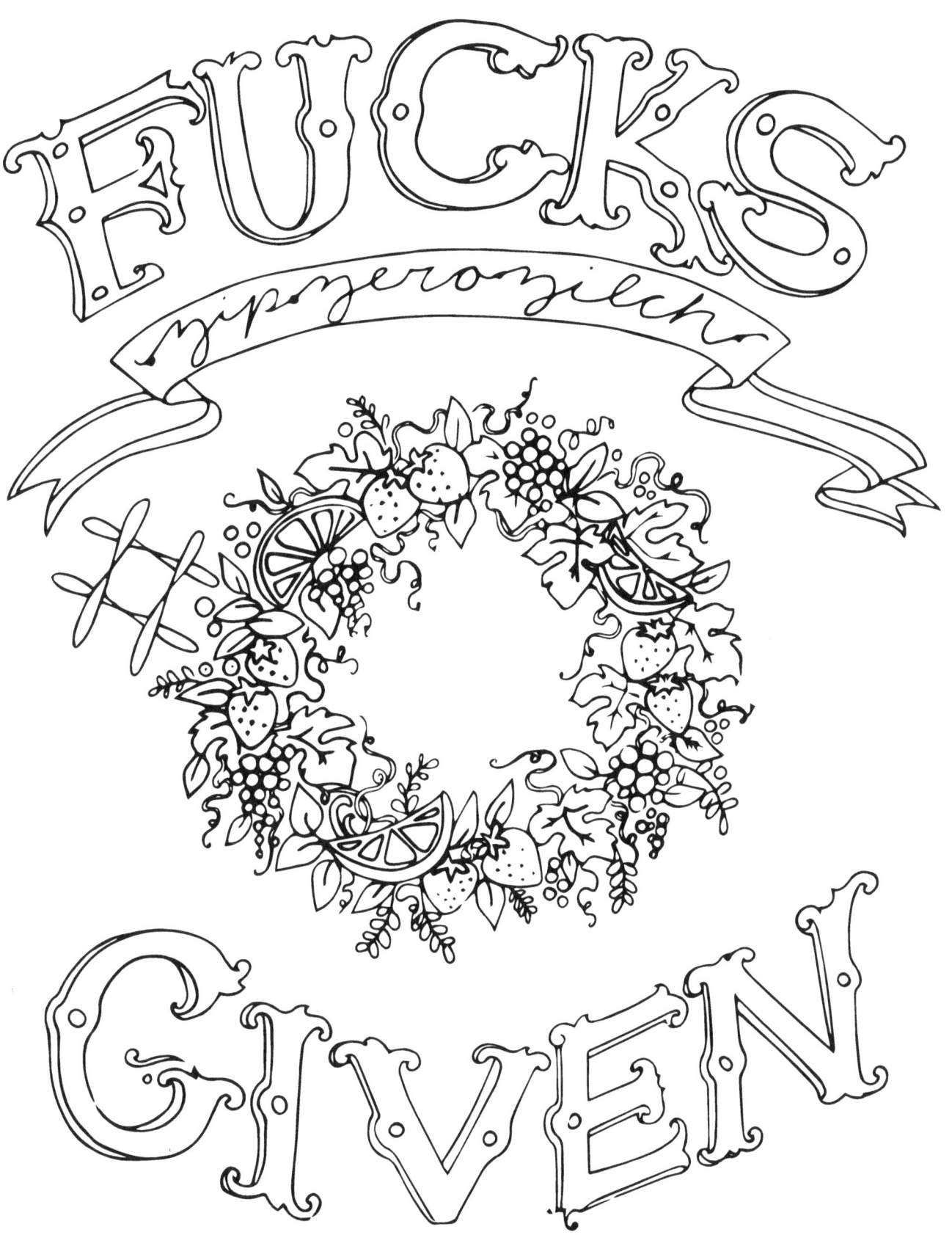

See previous...

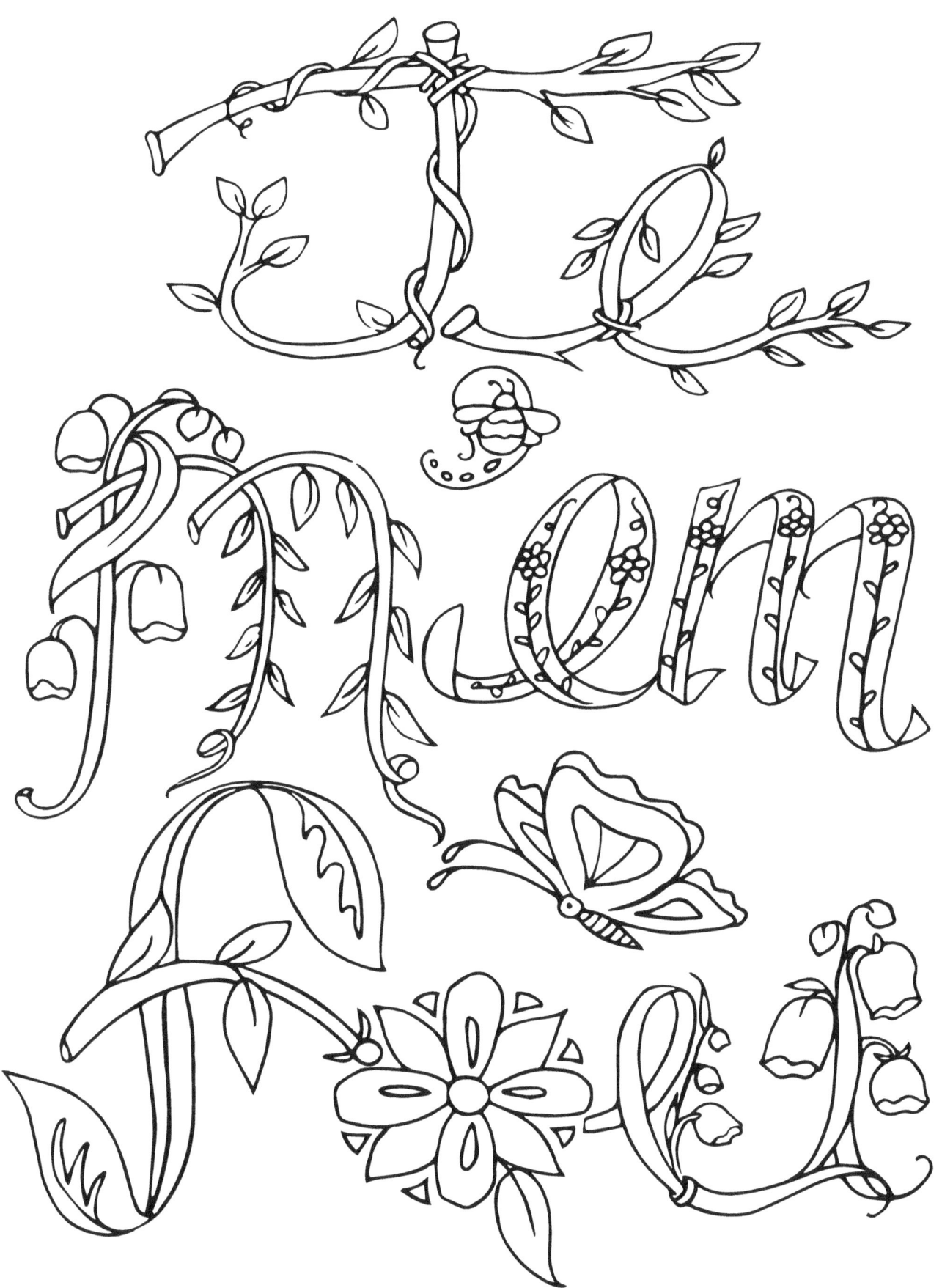

With toast...

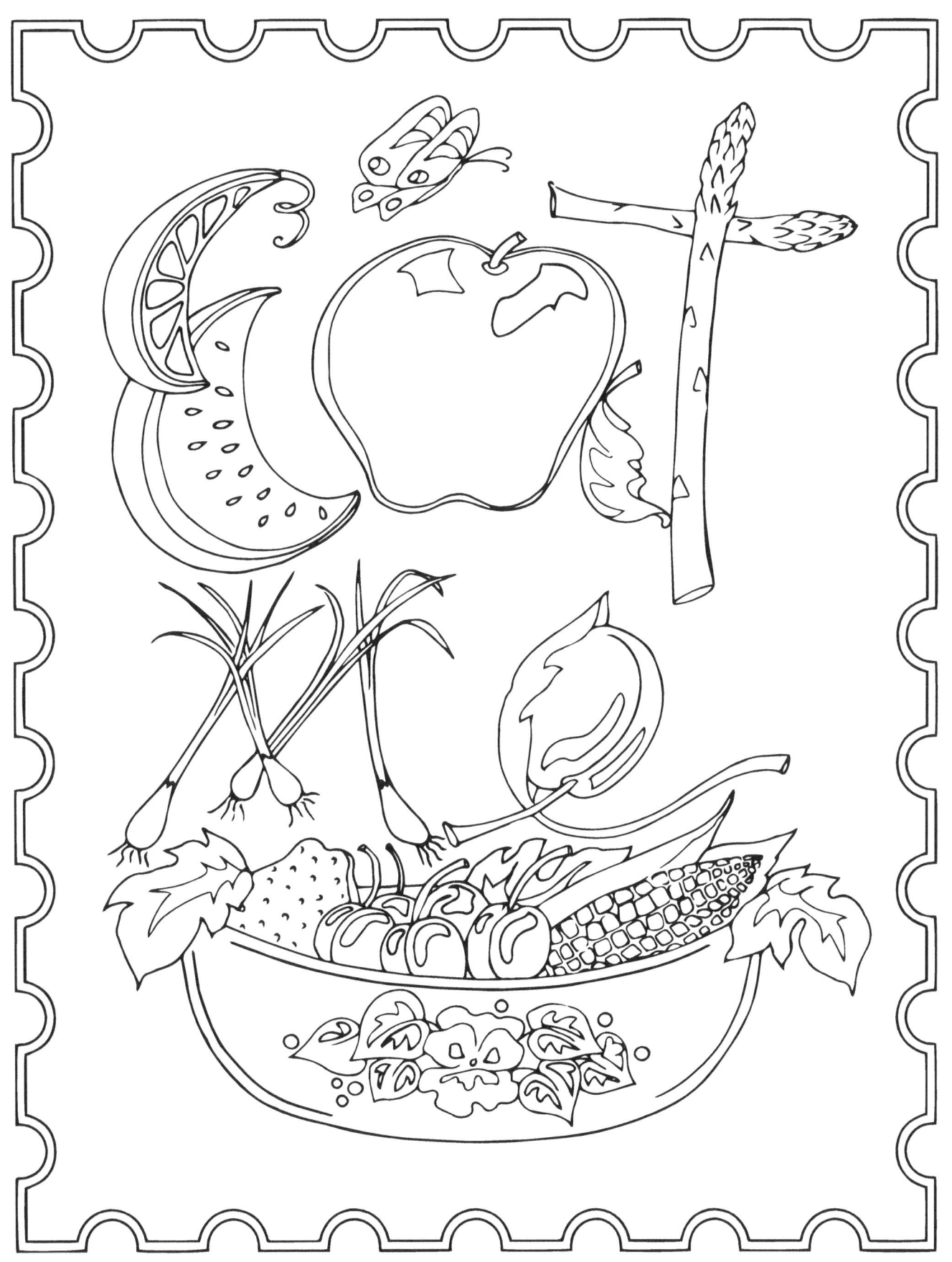

And jam...

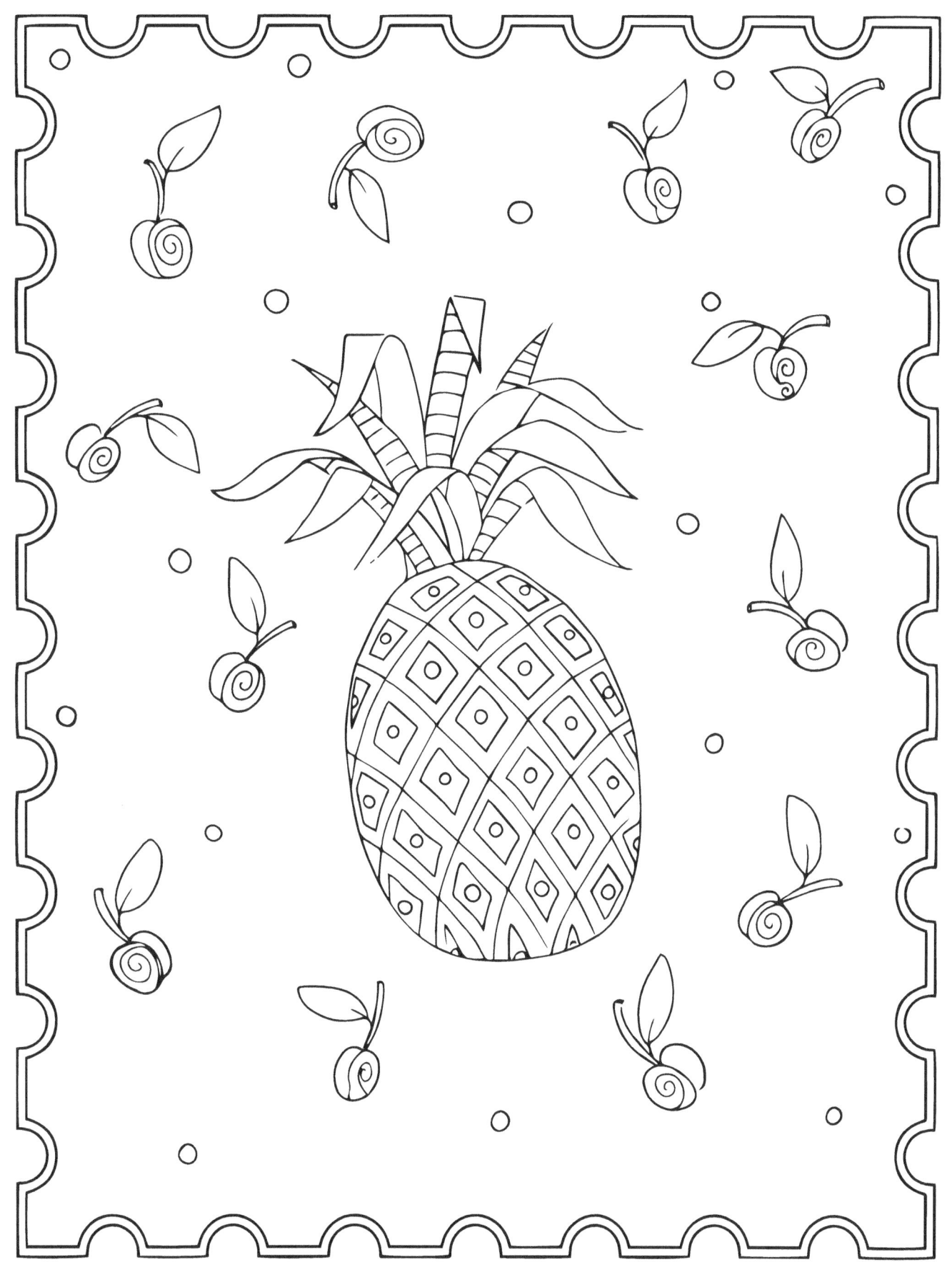

A face only a motherfucker could love...

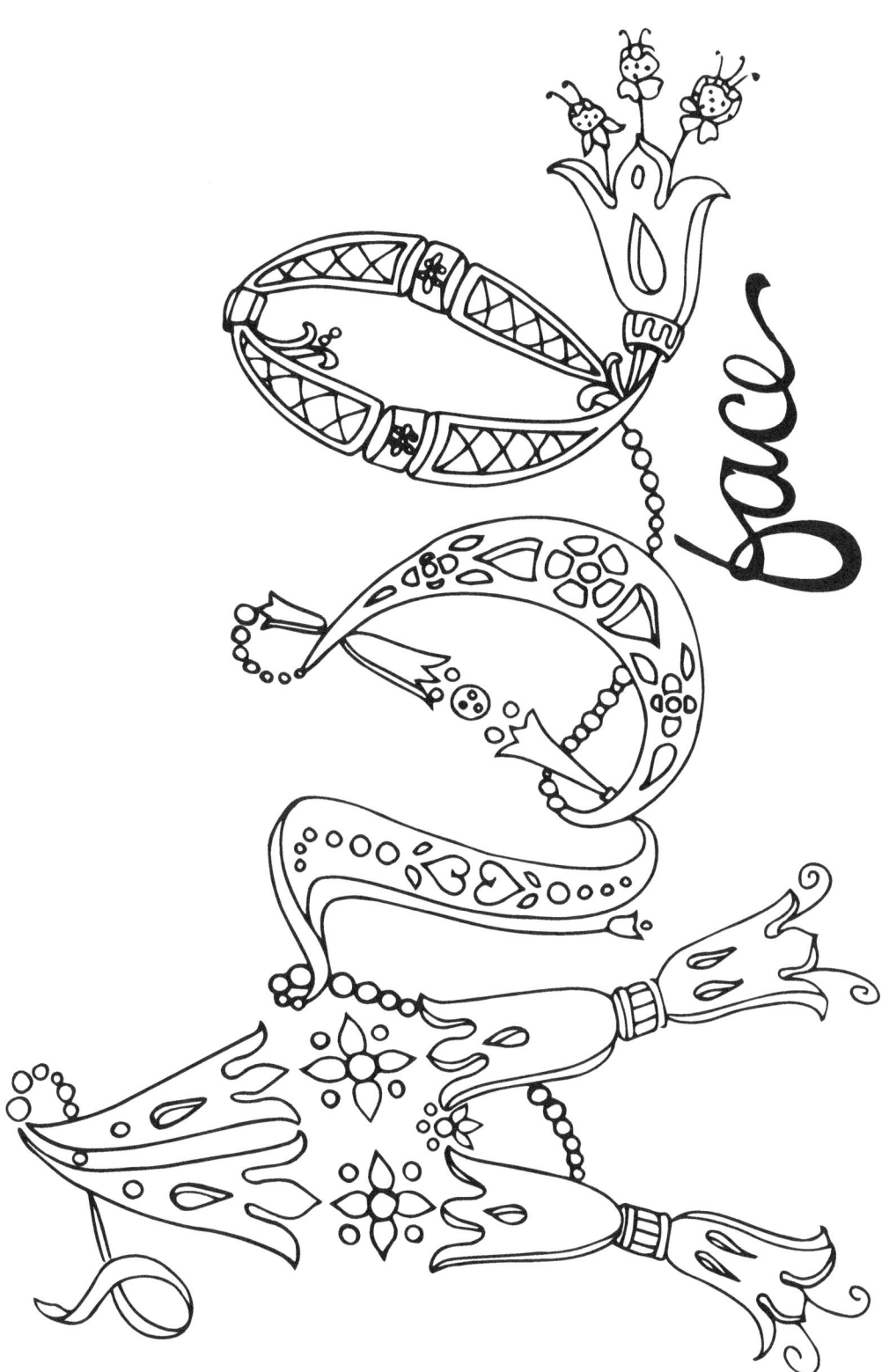

Self explanatory...

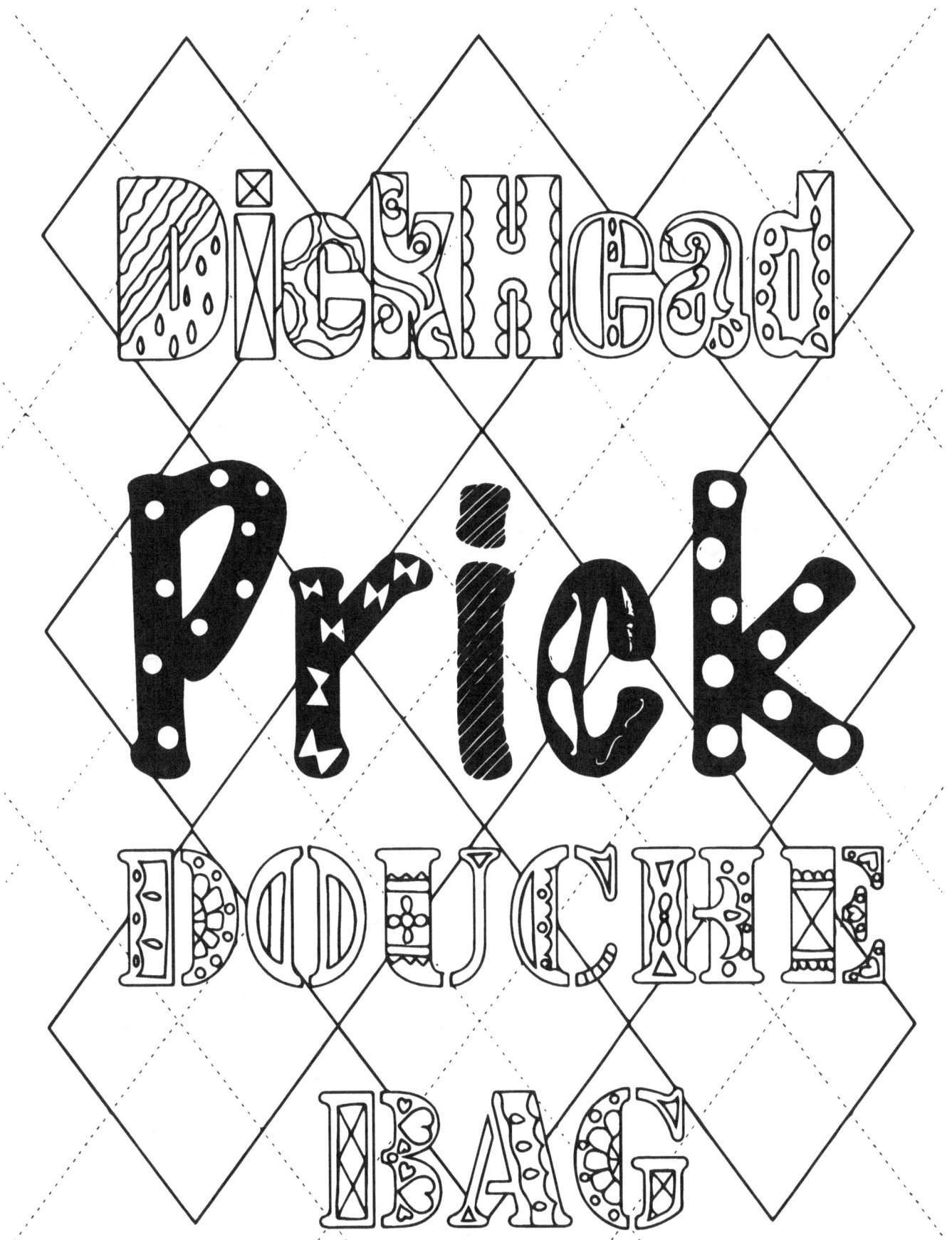

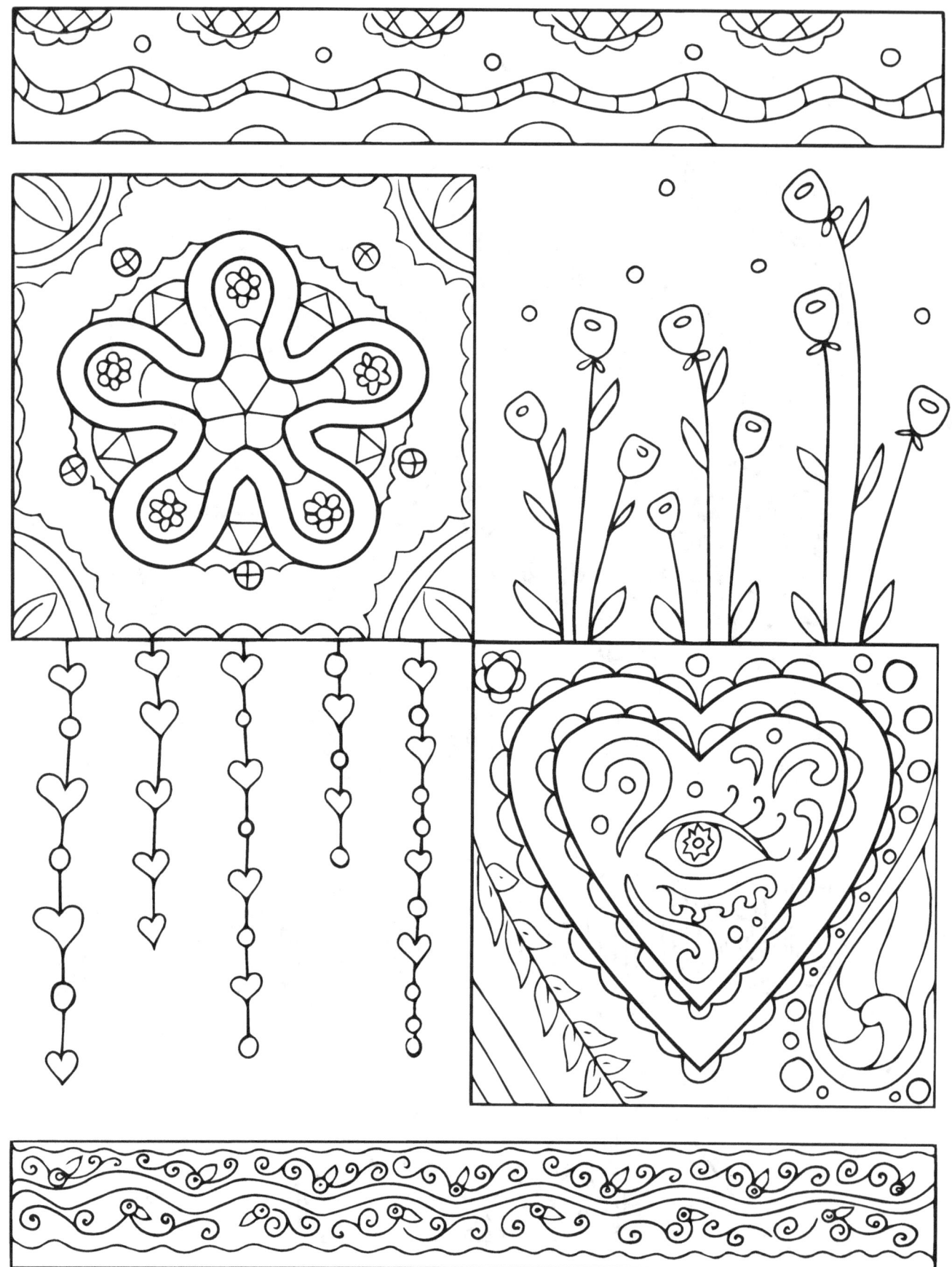

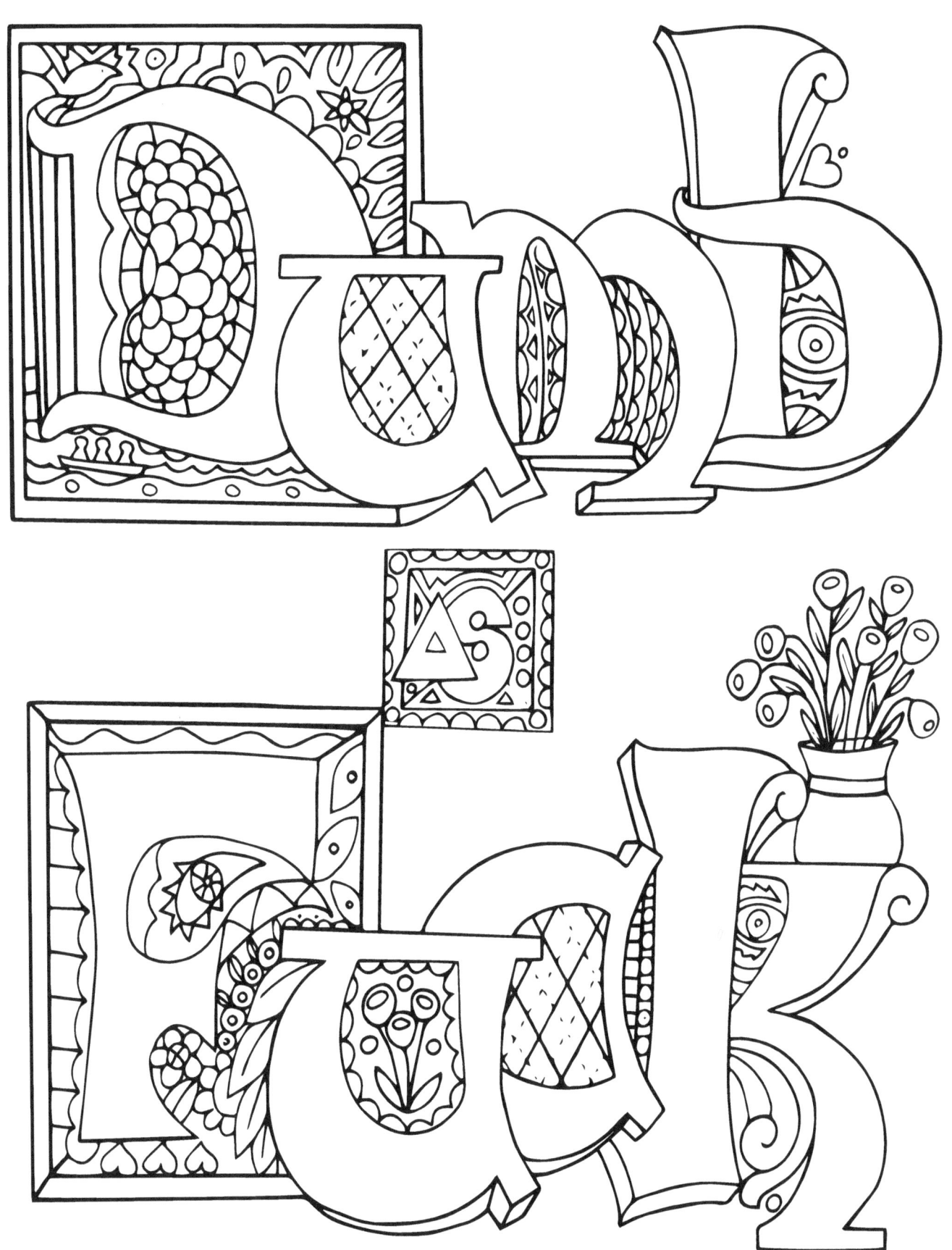

Dumb as fuck

Sometimes, less is more...

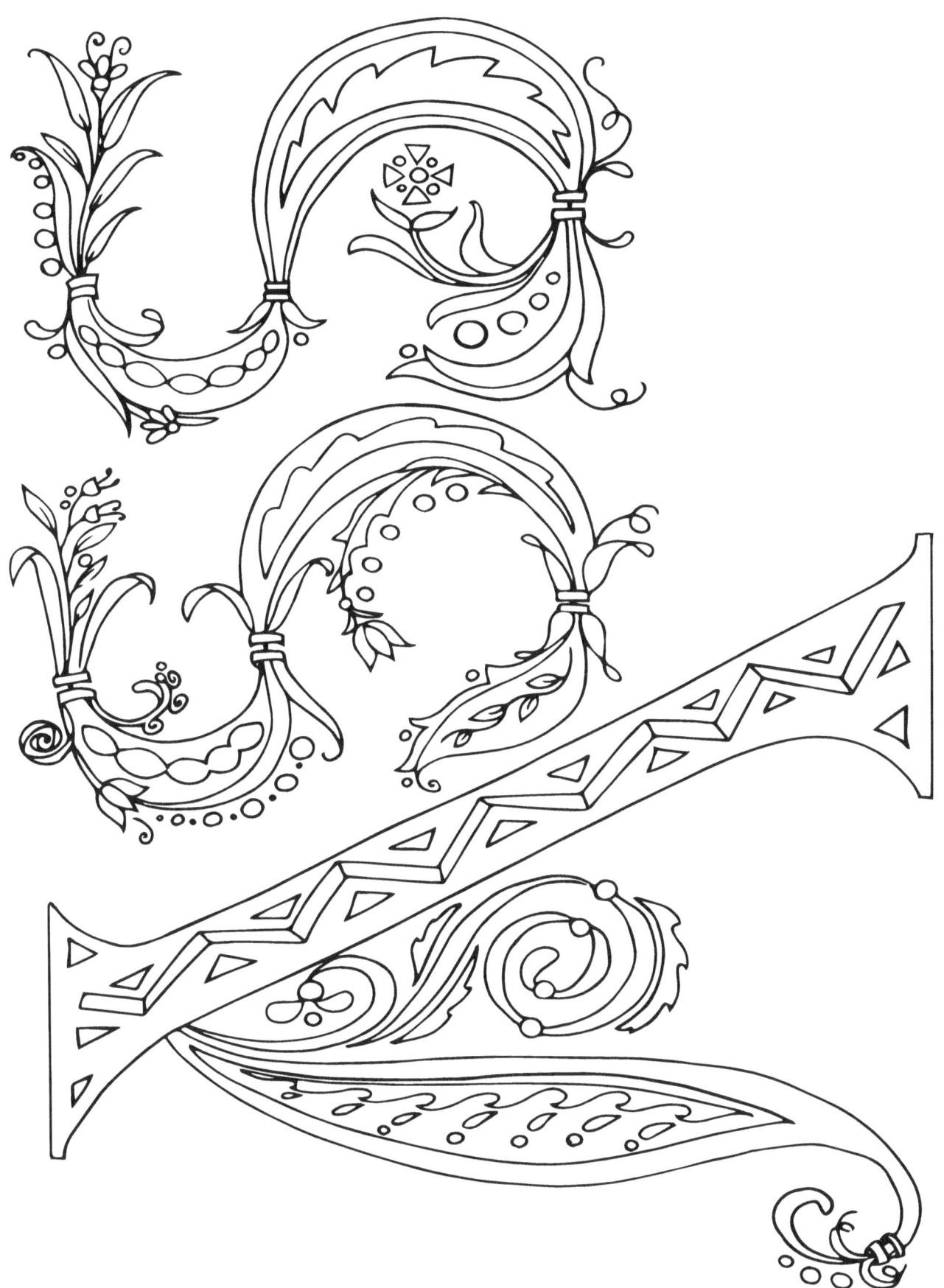

We've had enough, thanks...

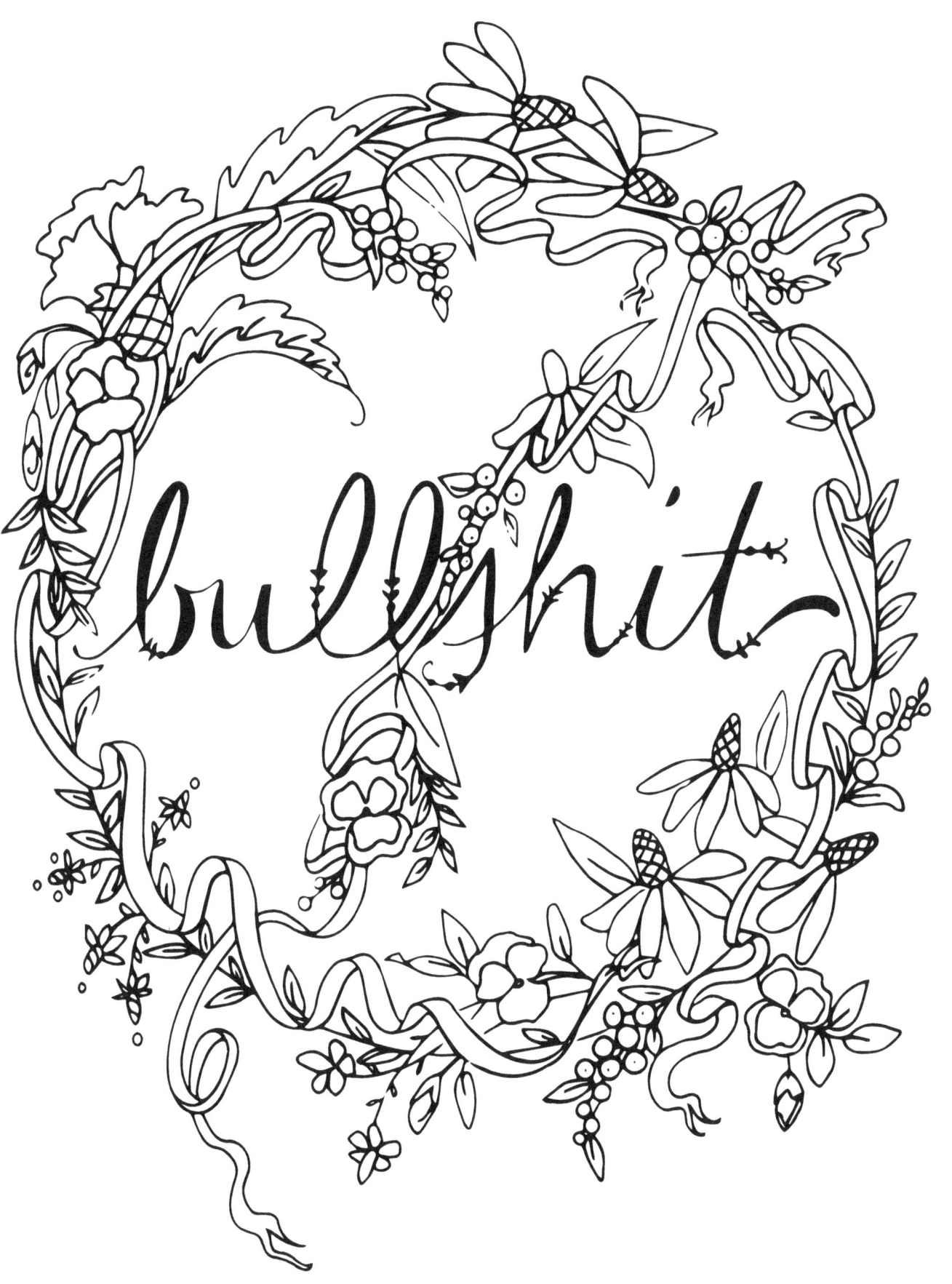

Yep, you read that right...

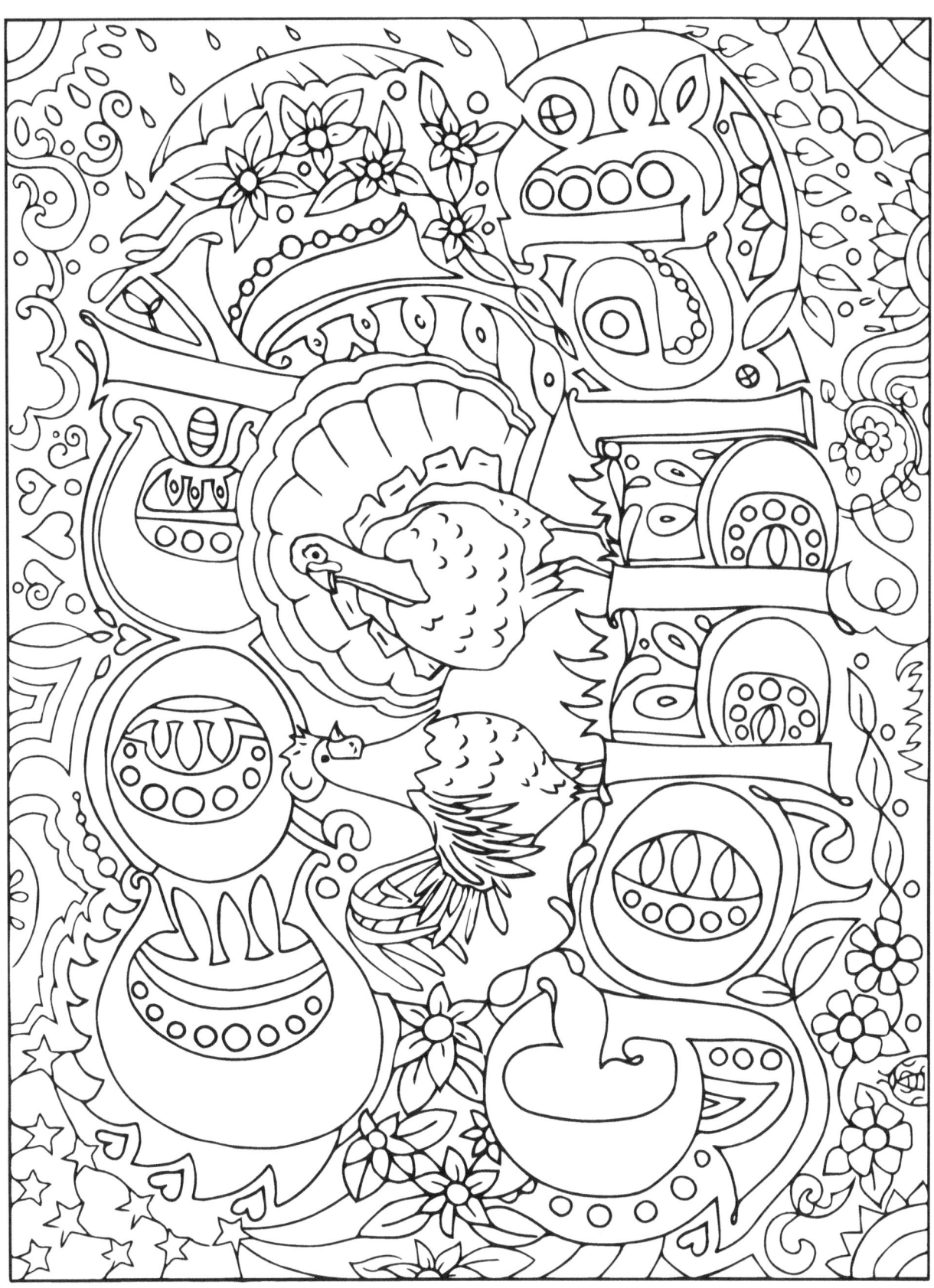

C U next Tuesday, Yes?

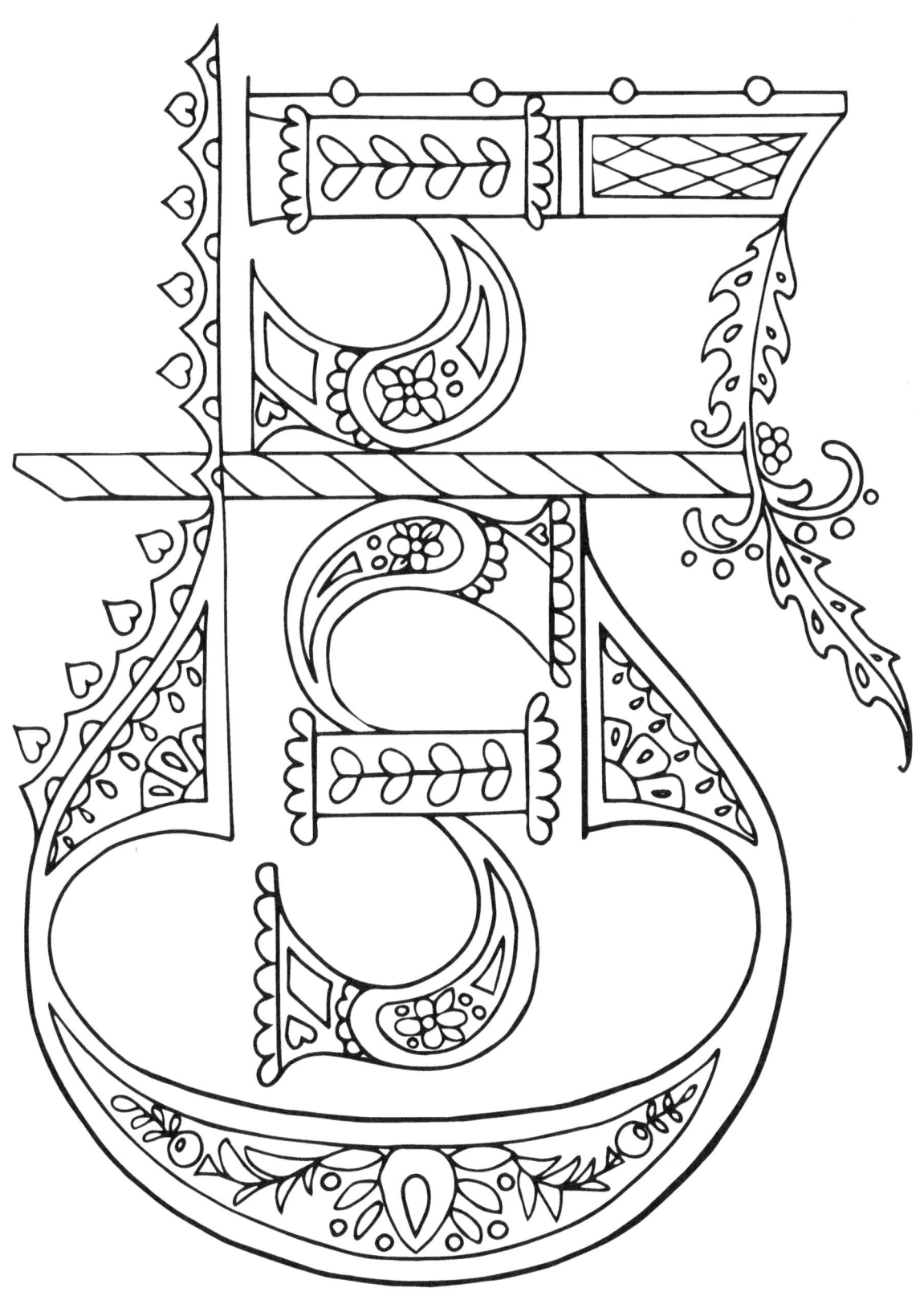

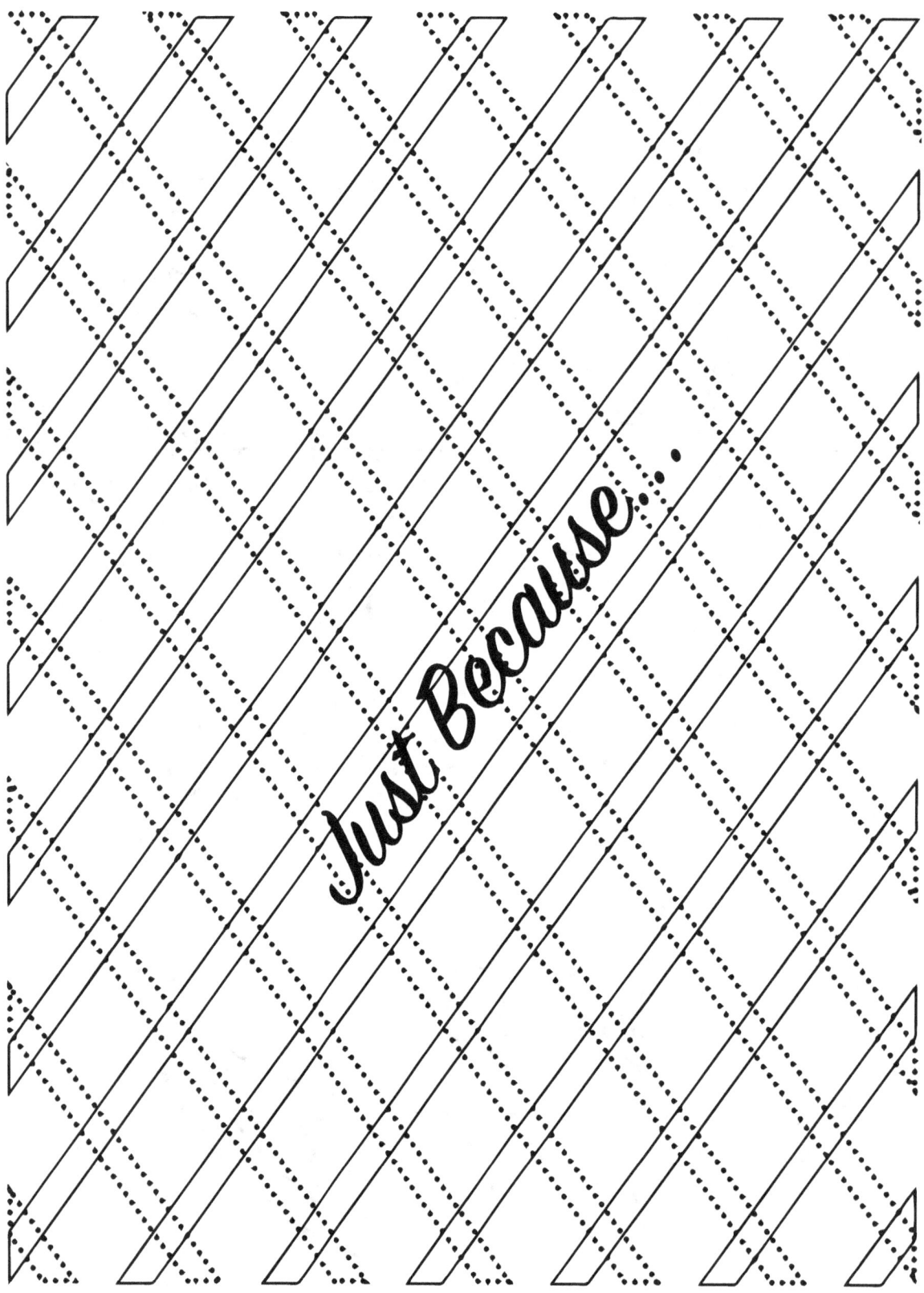

Just Because....

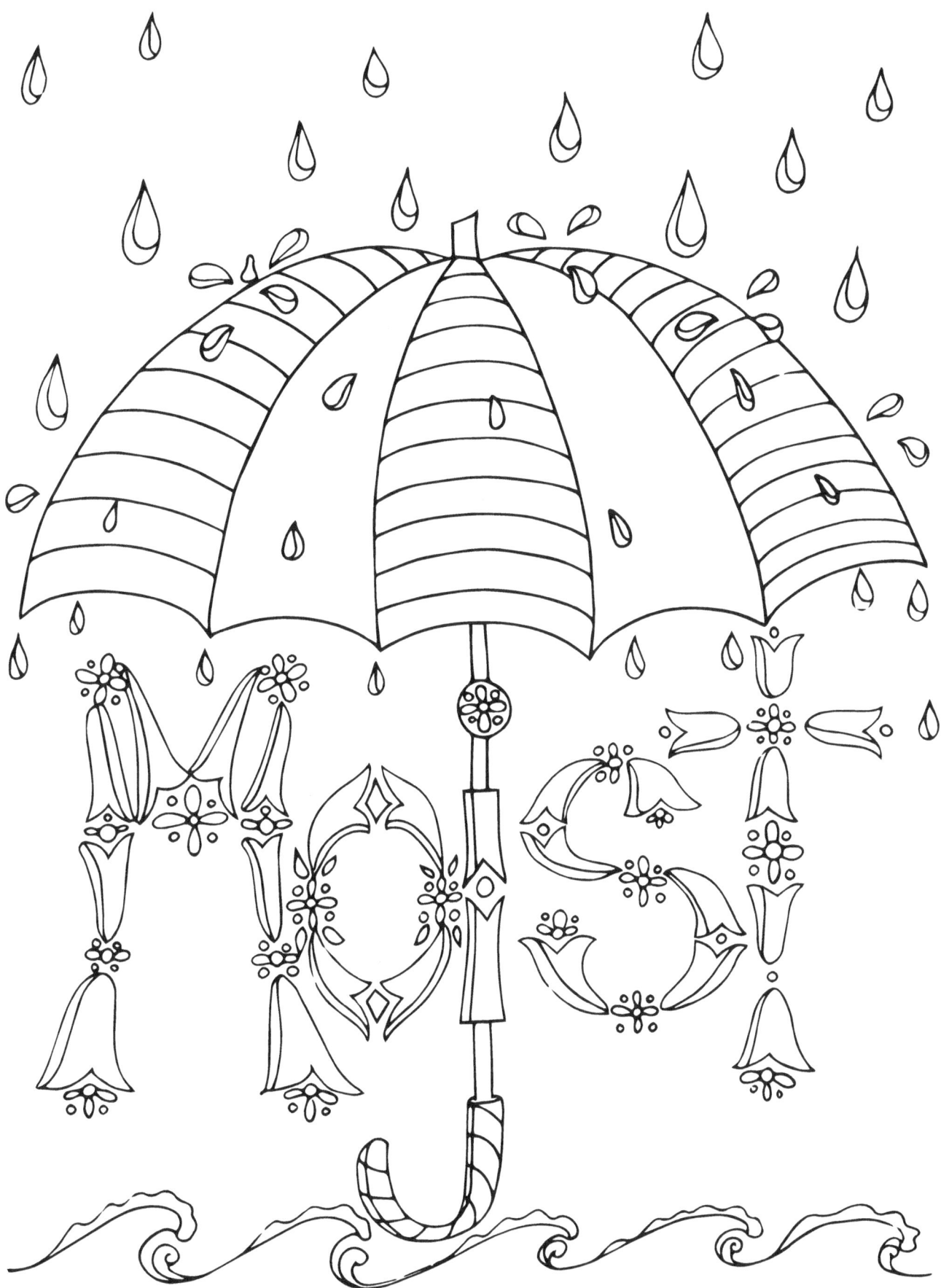

You know you wanna...

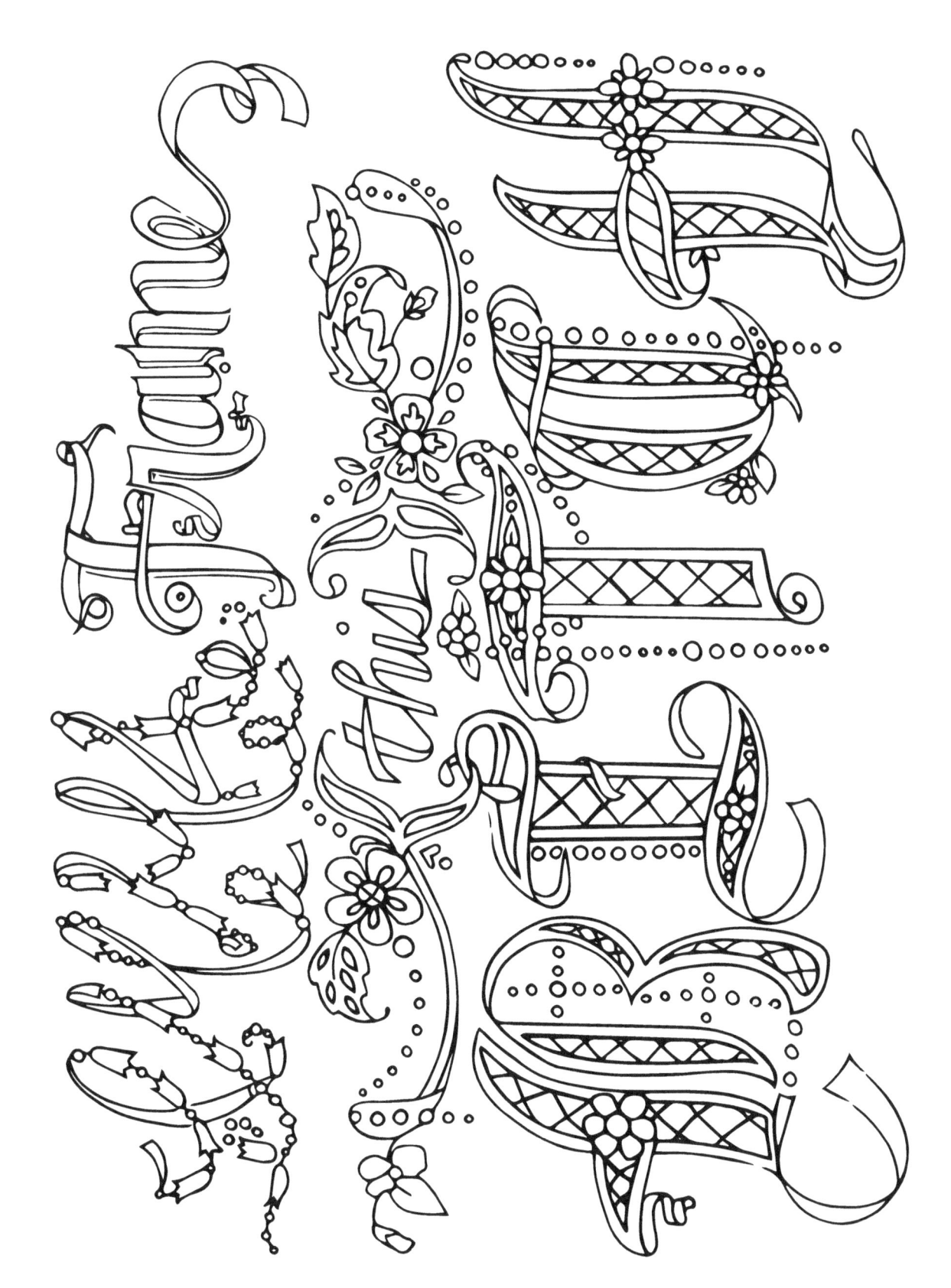

?

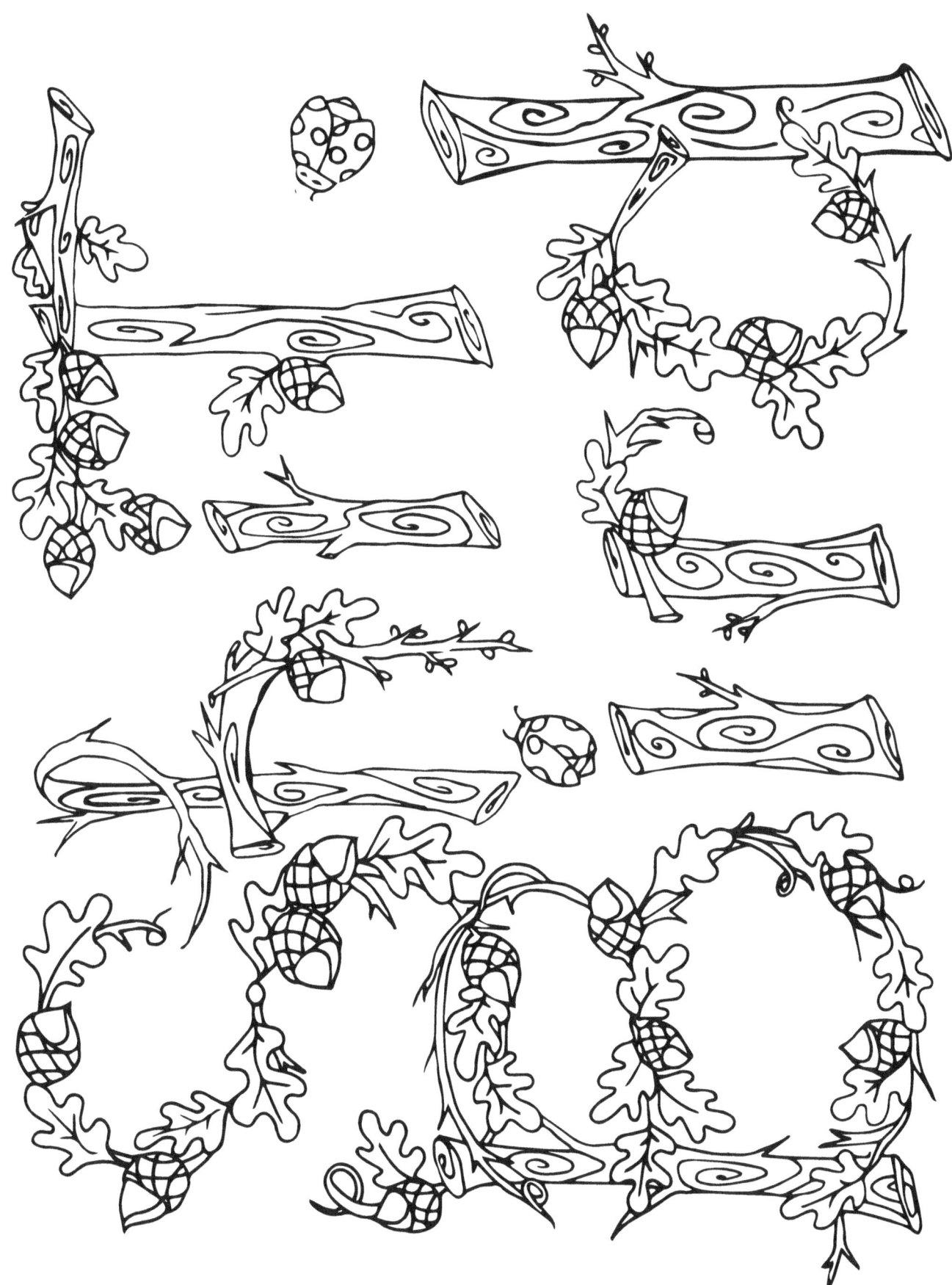

Sans Nuts...

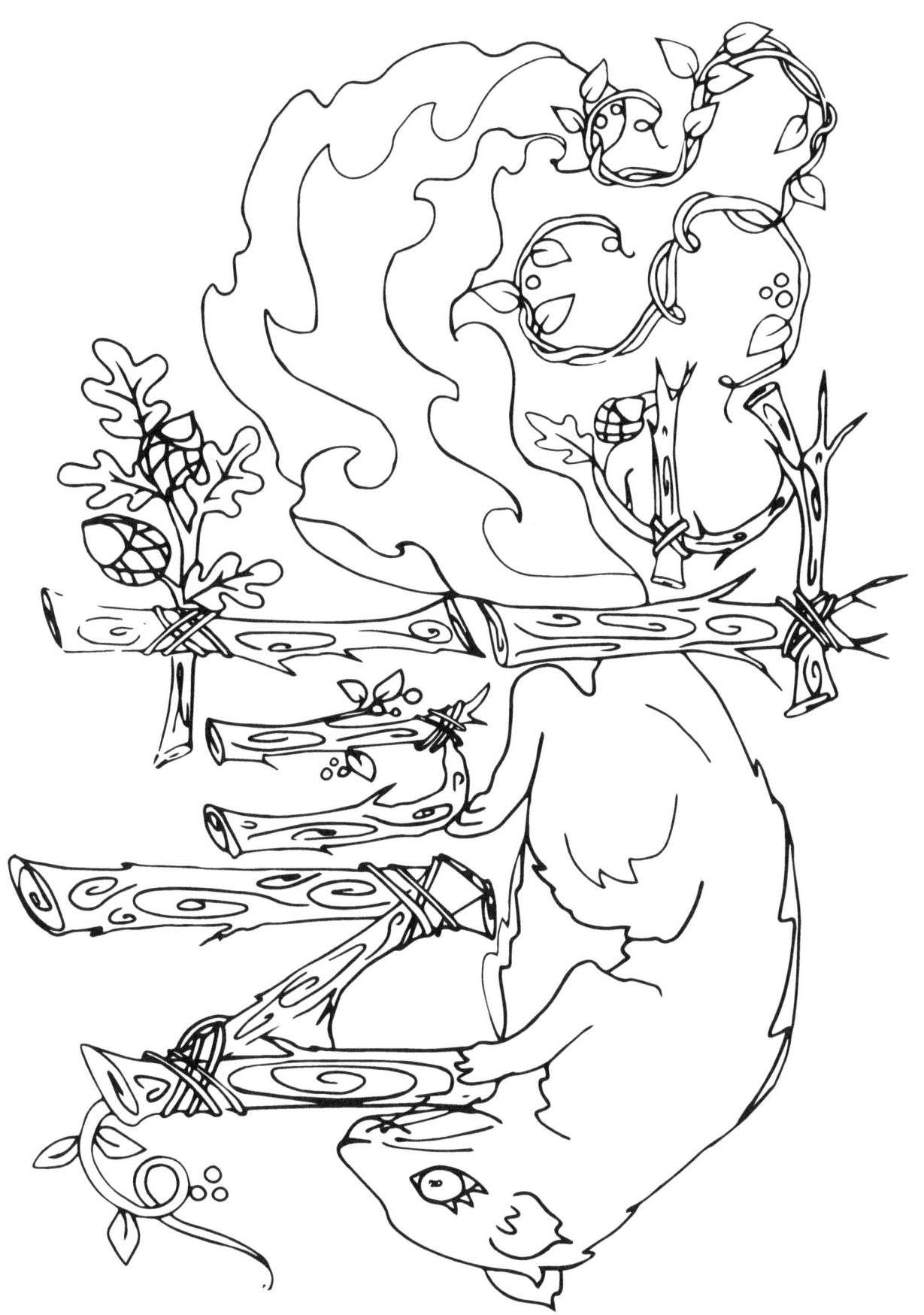

Alma Mater...

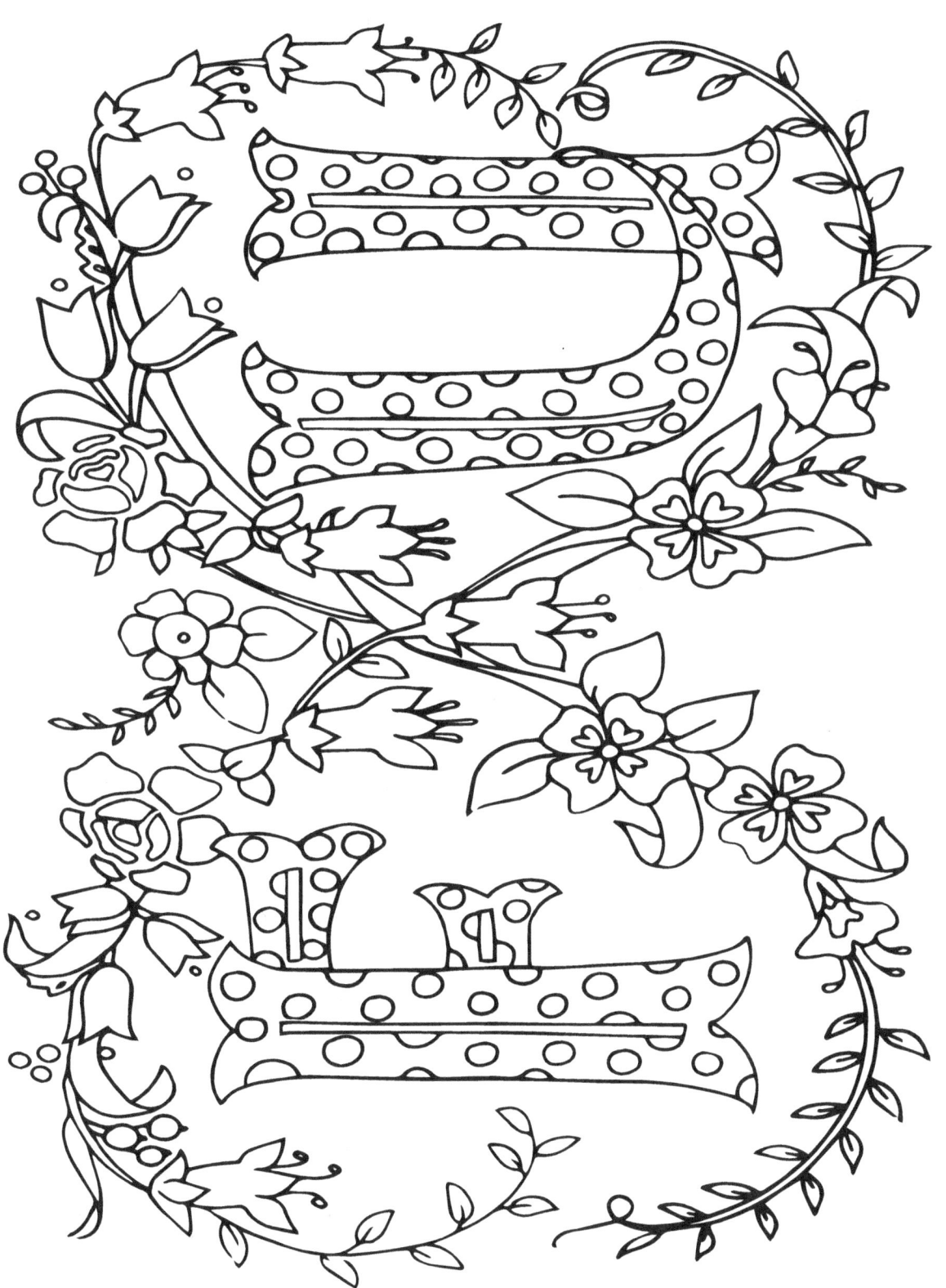

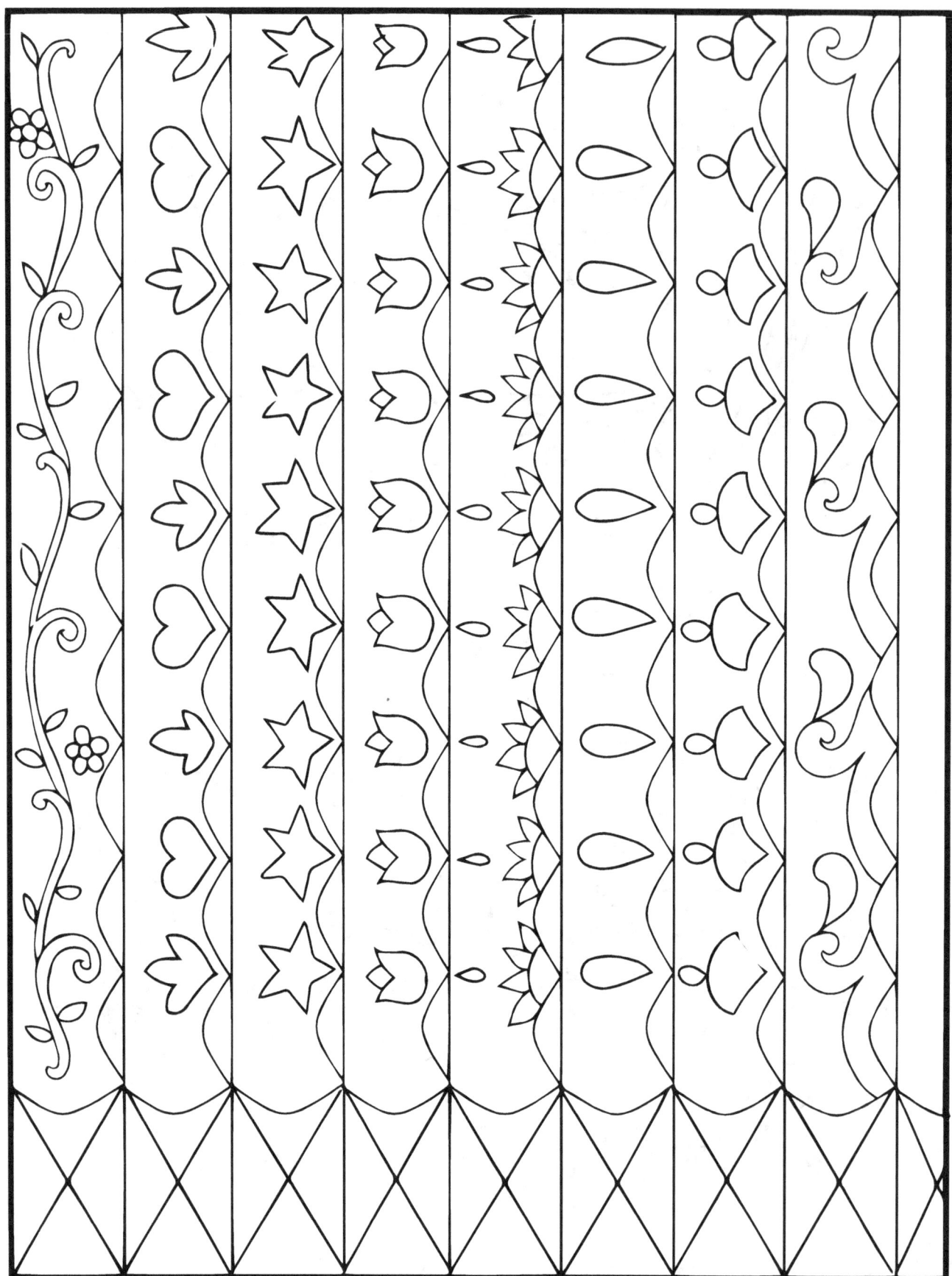

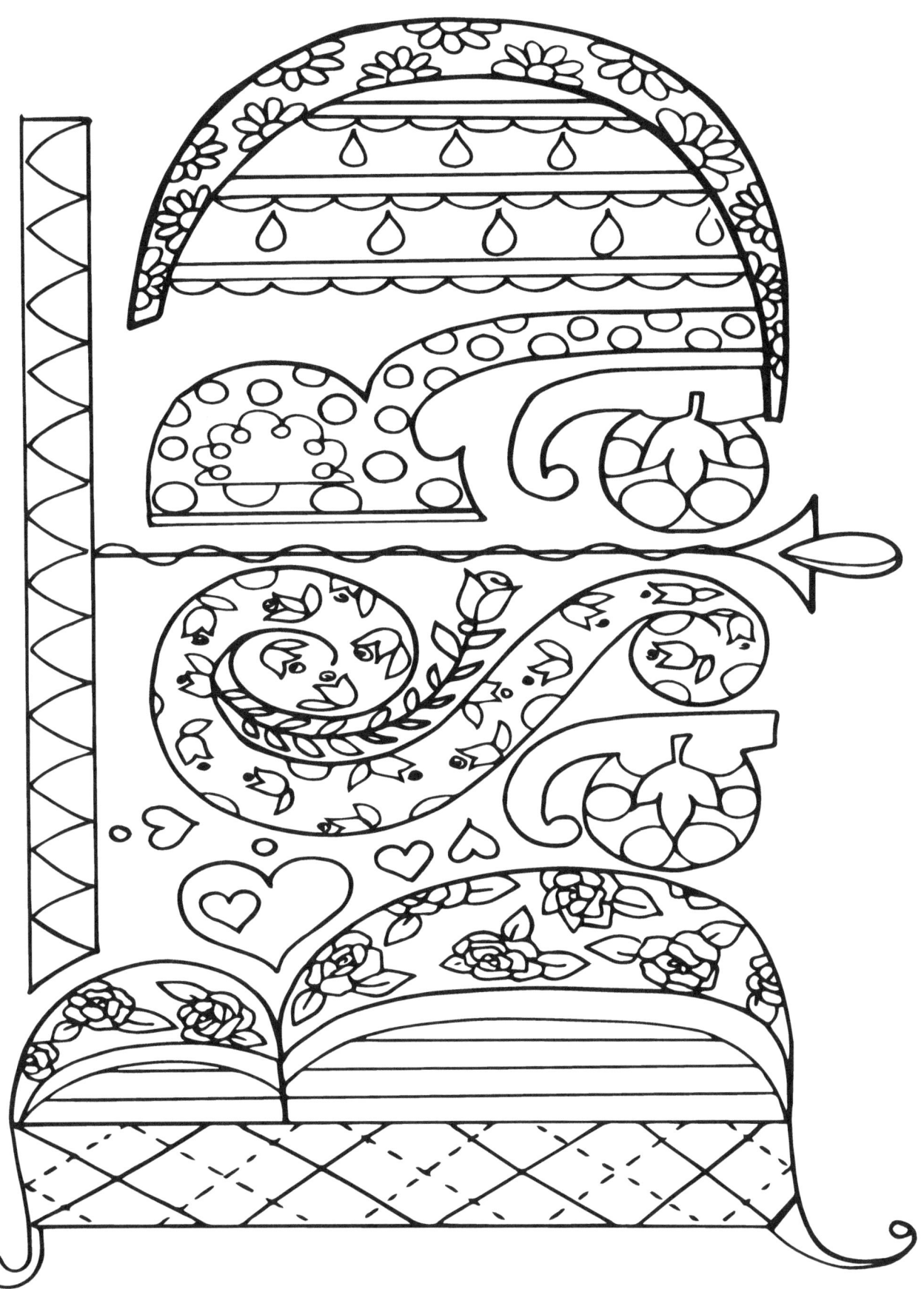

Complete...

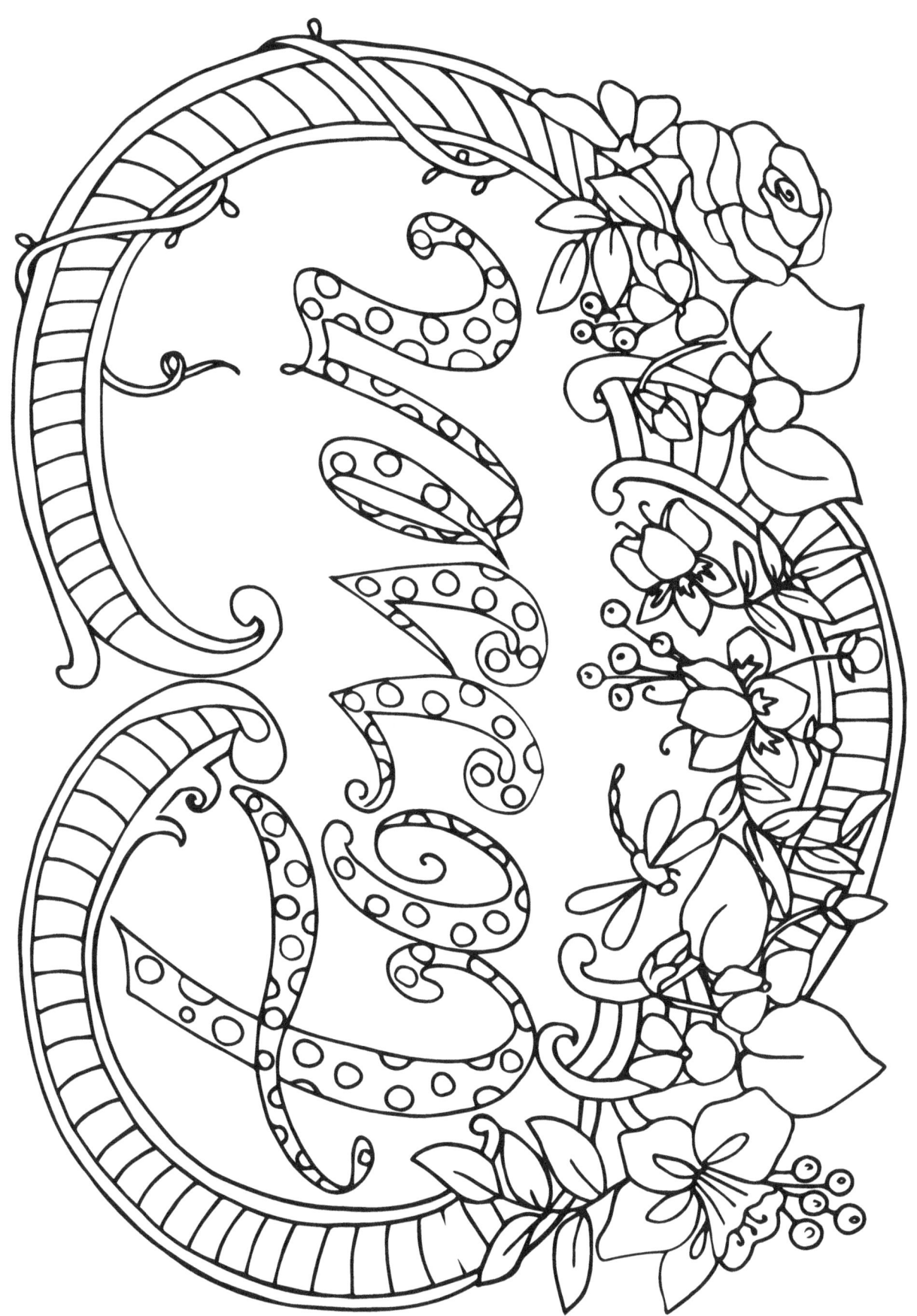

Utter...

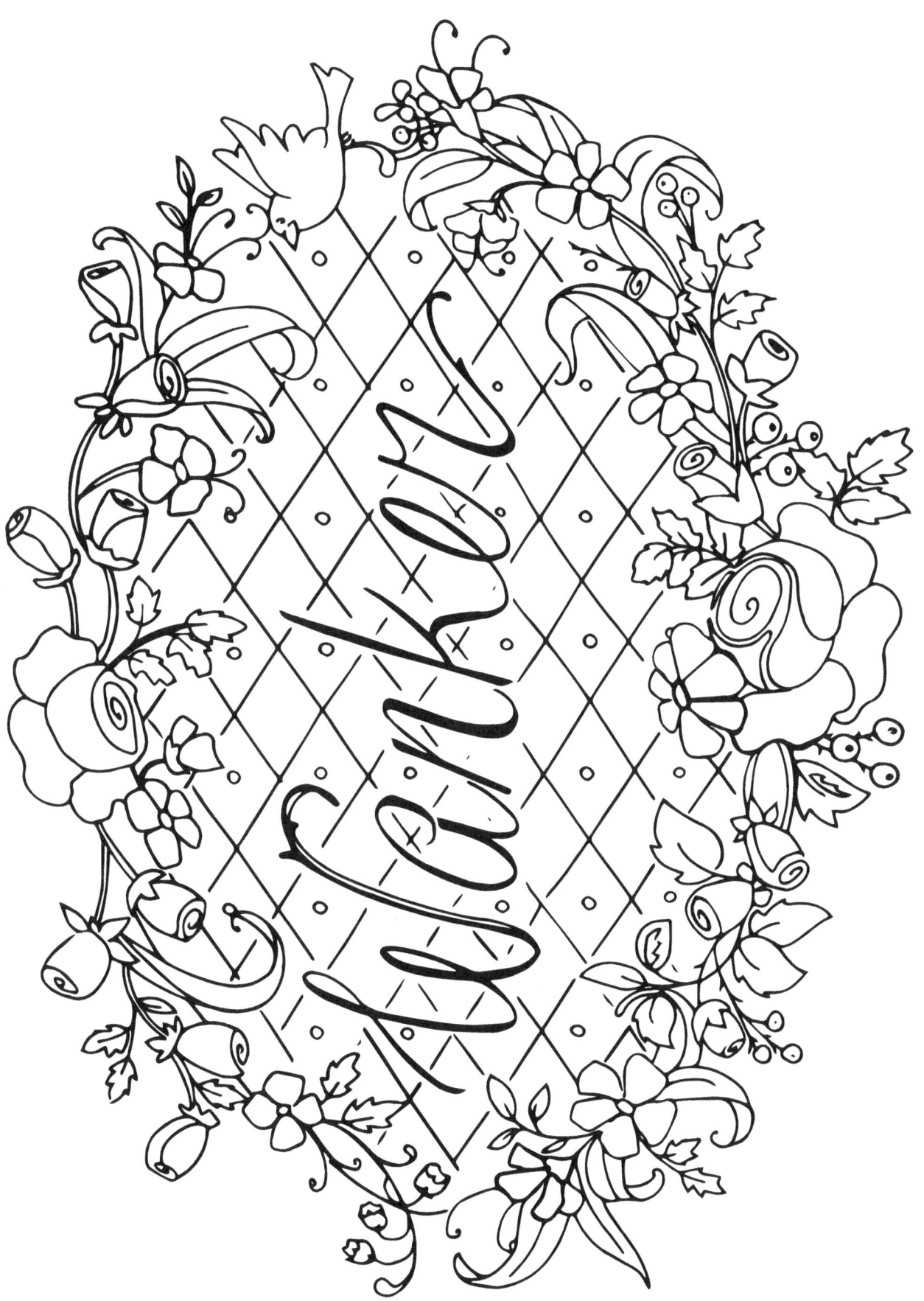

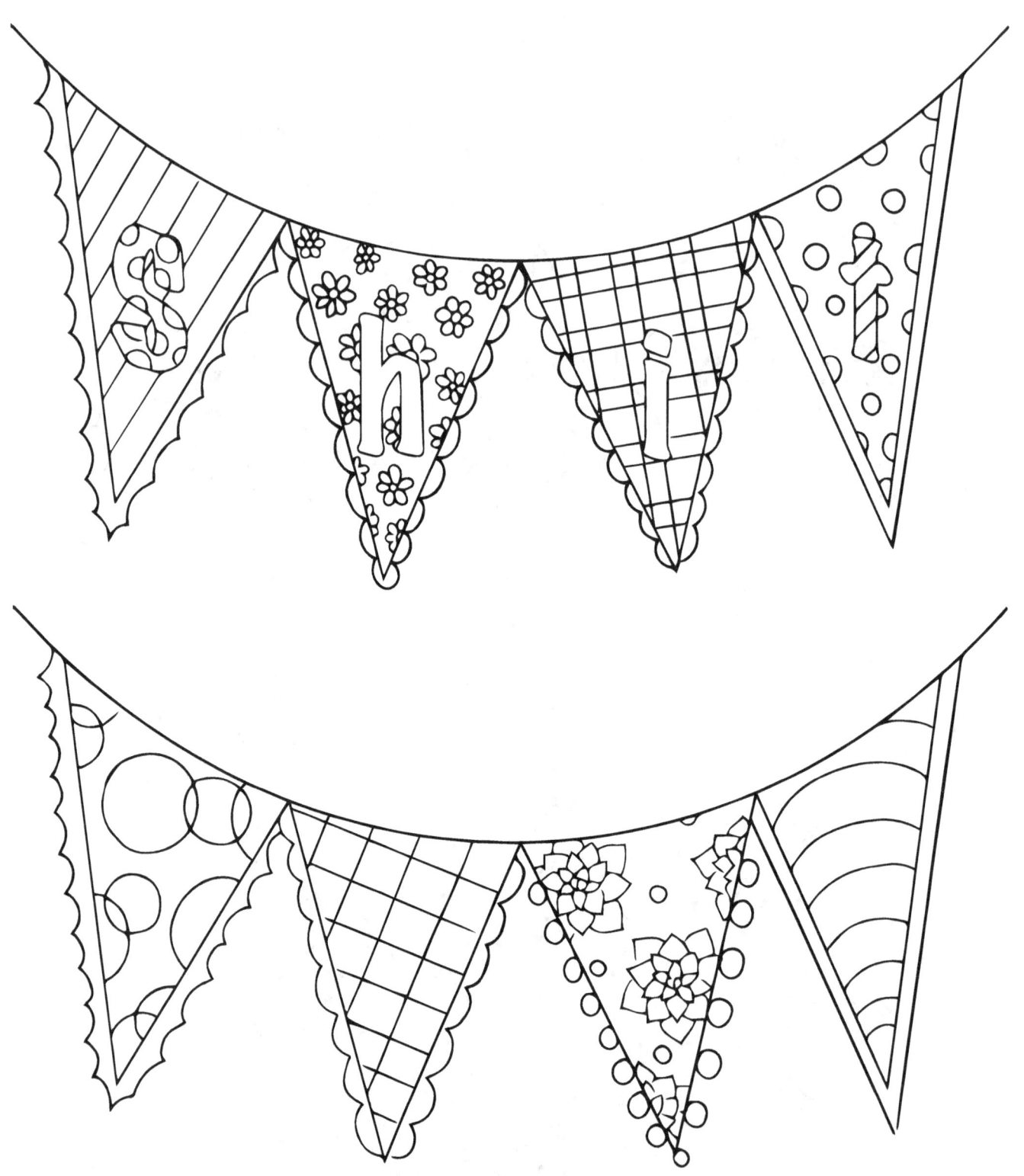

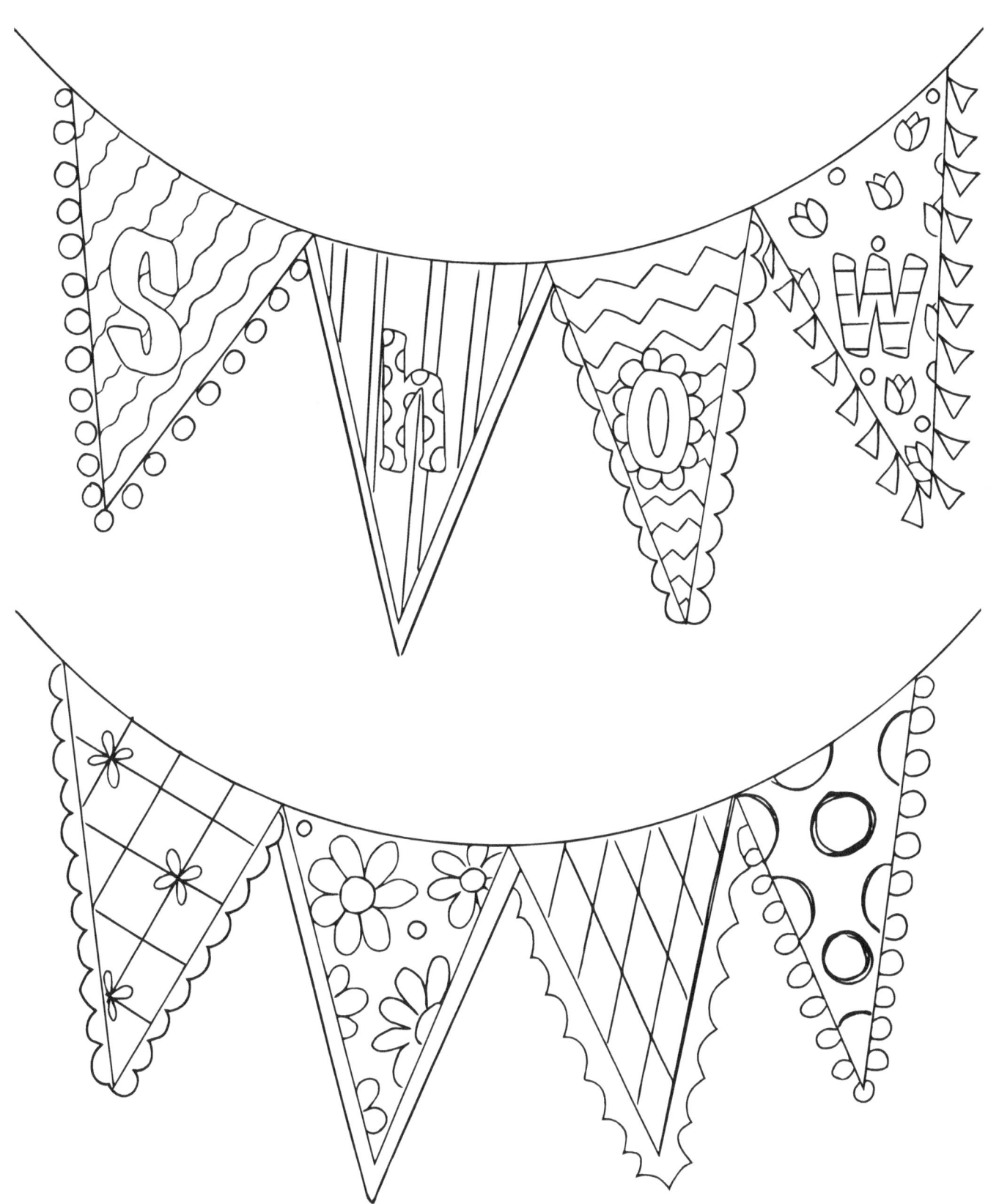

Should probably look into that...

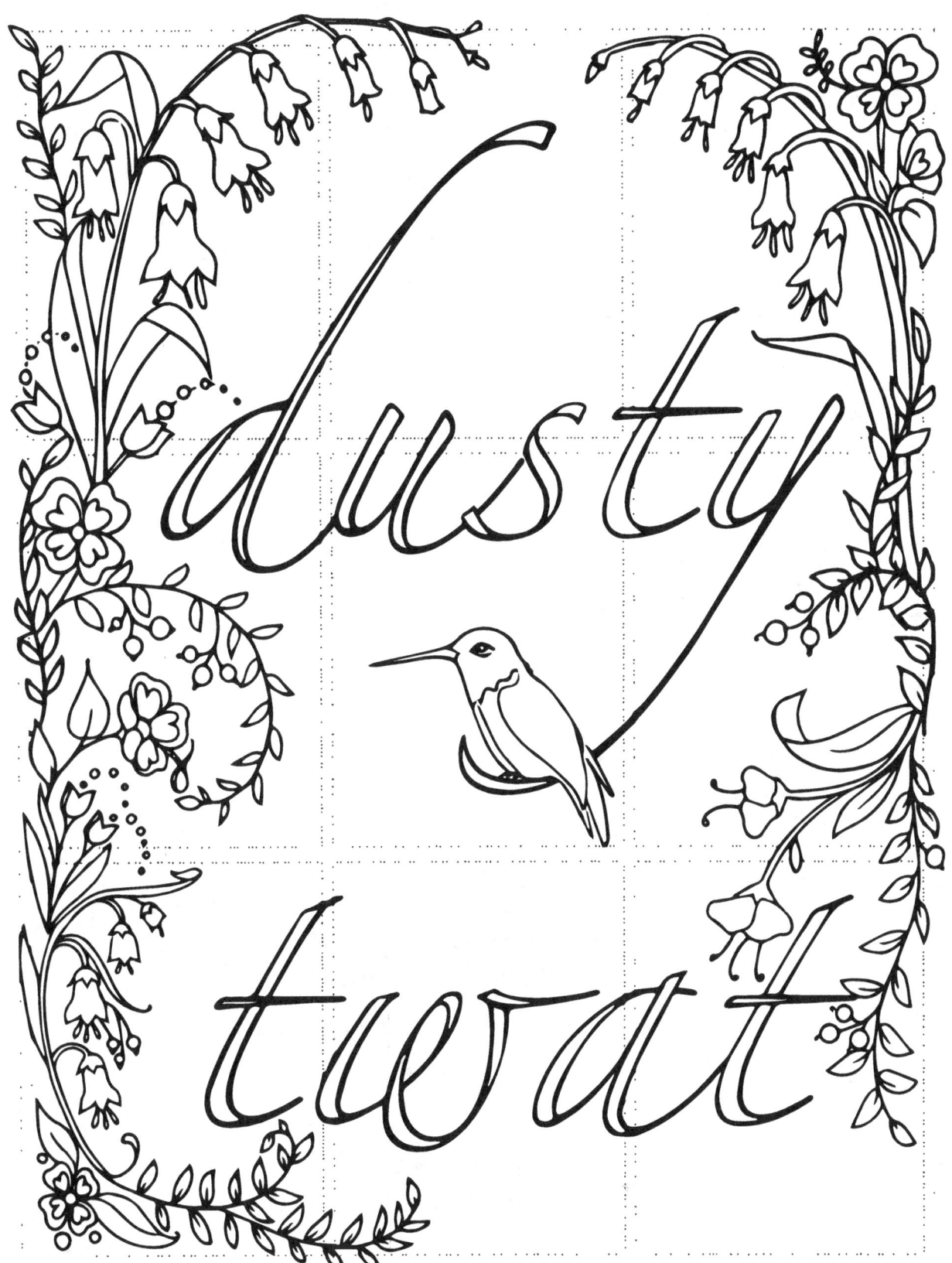

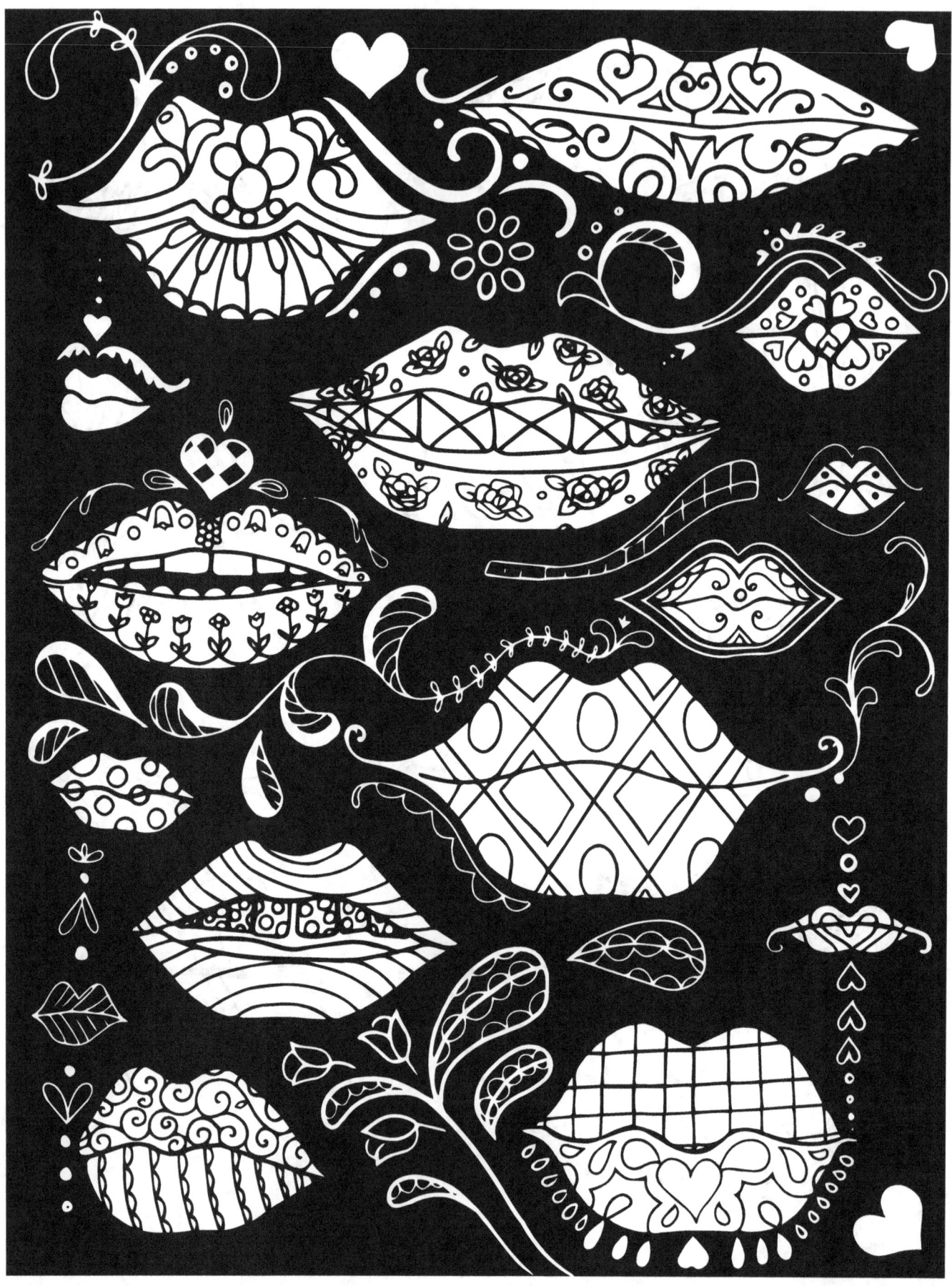

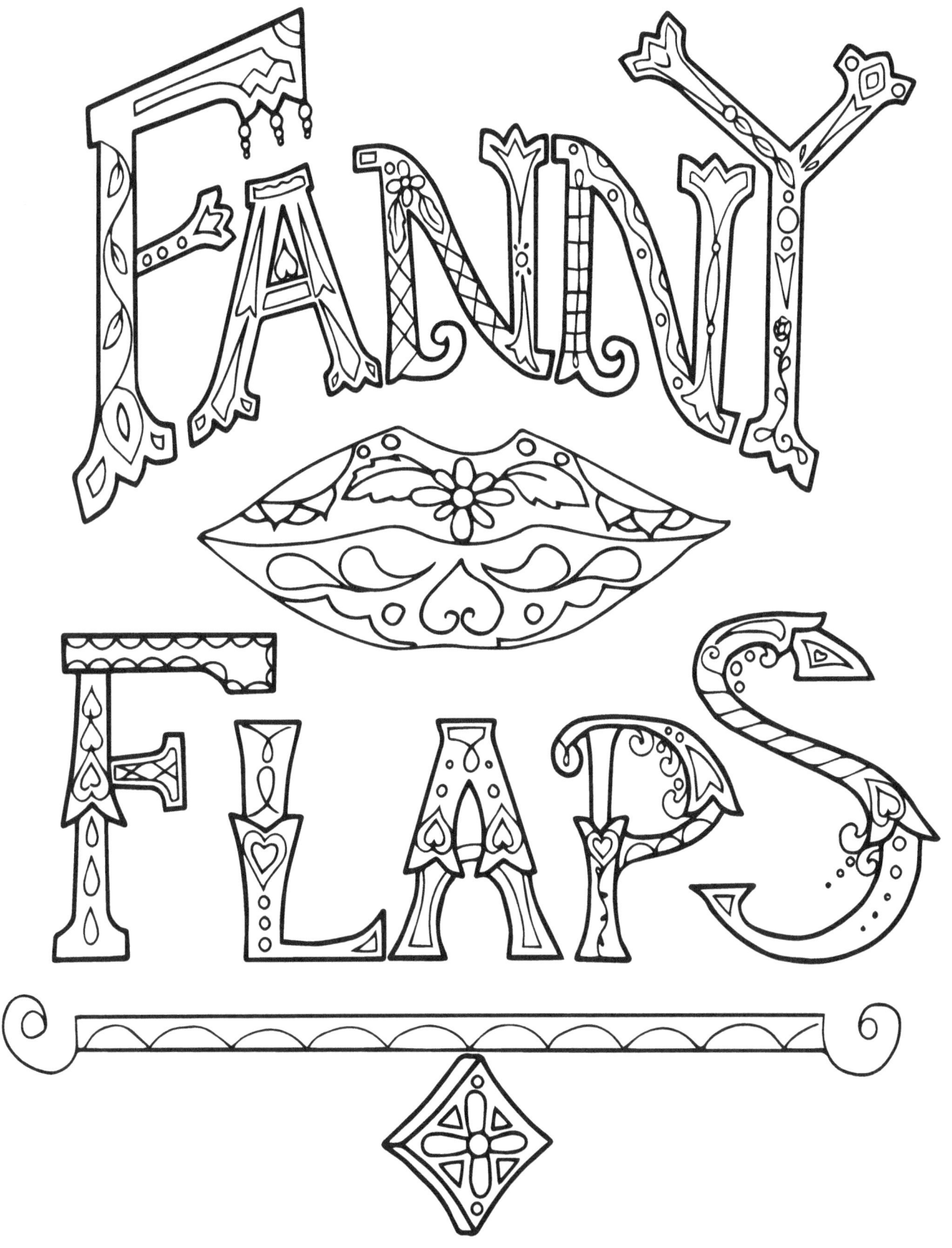

If you must...

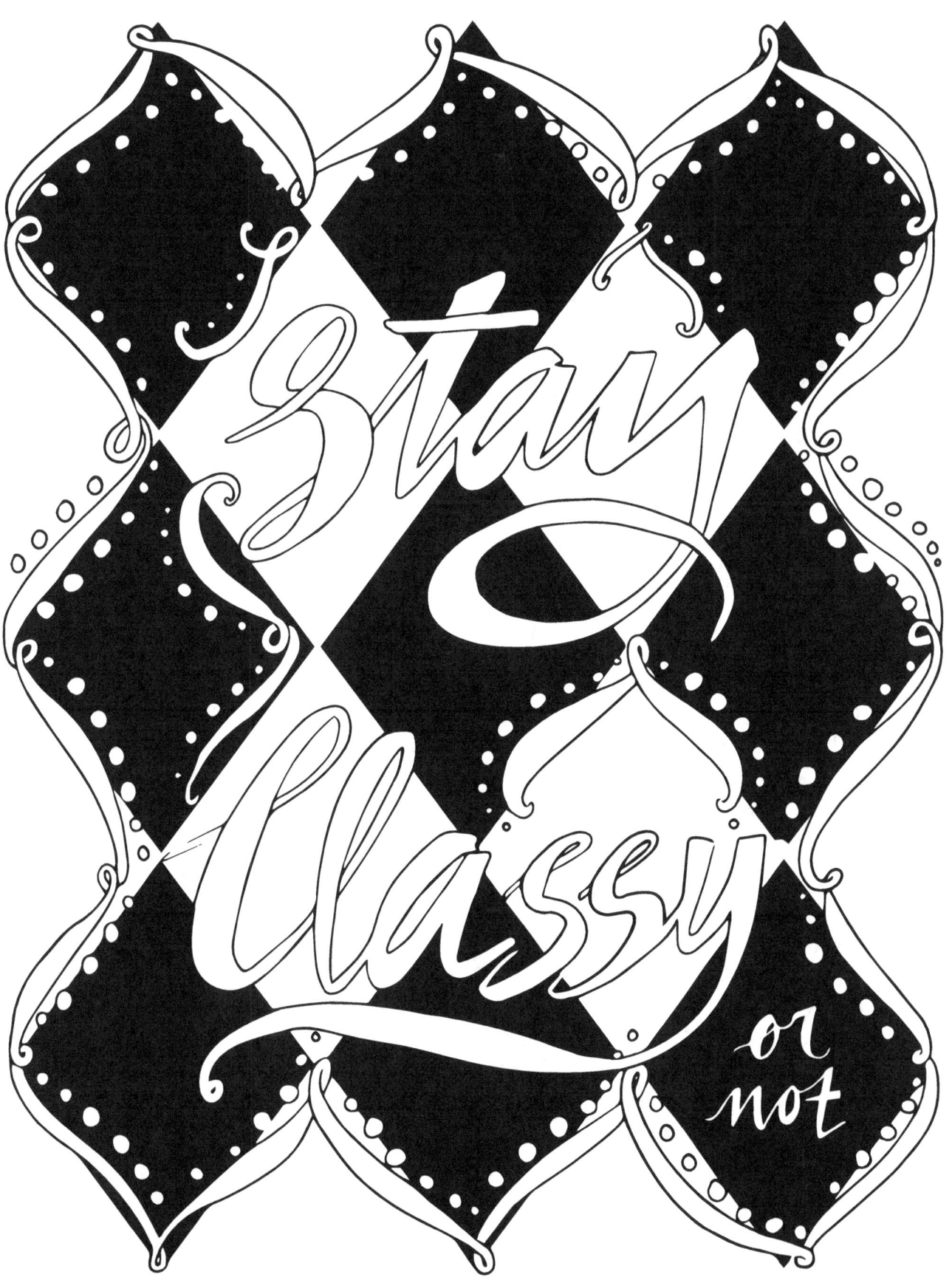

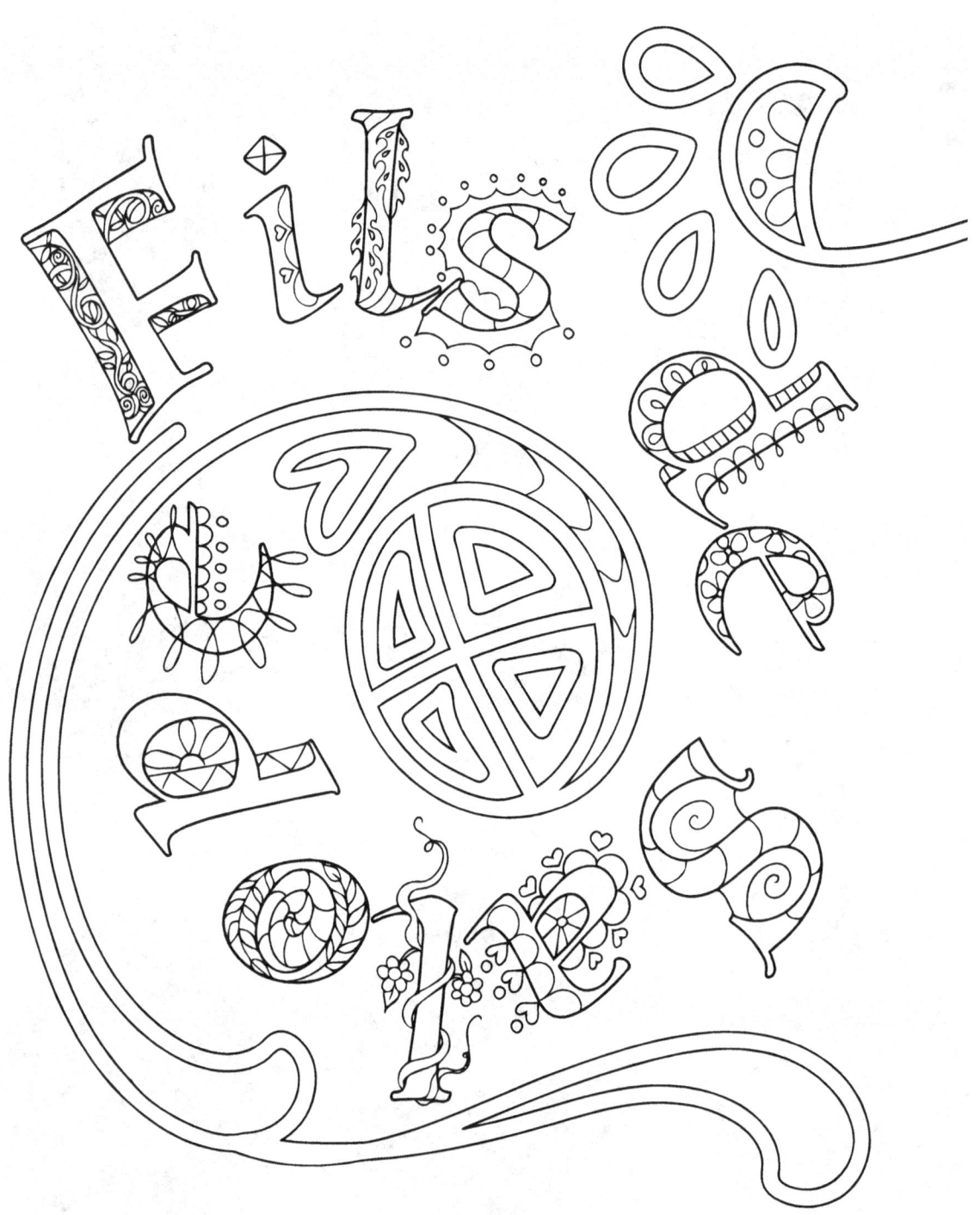

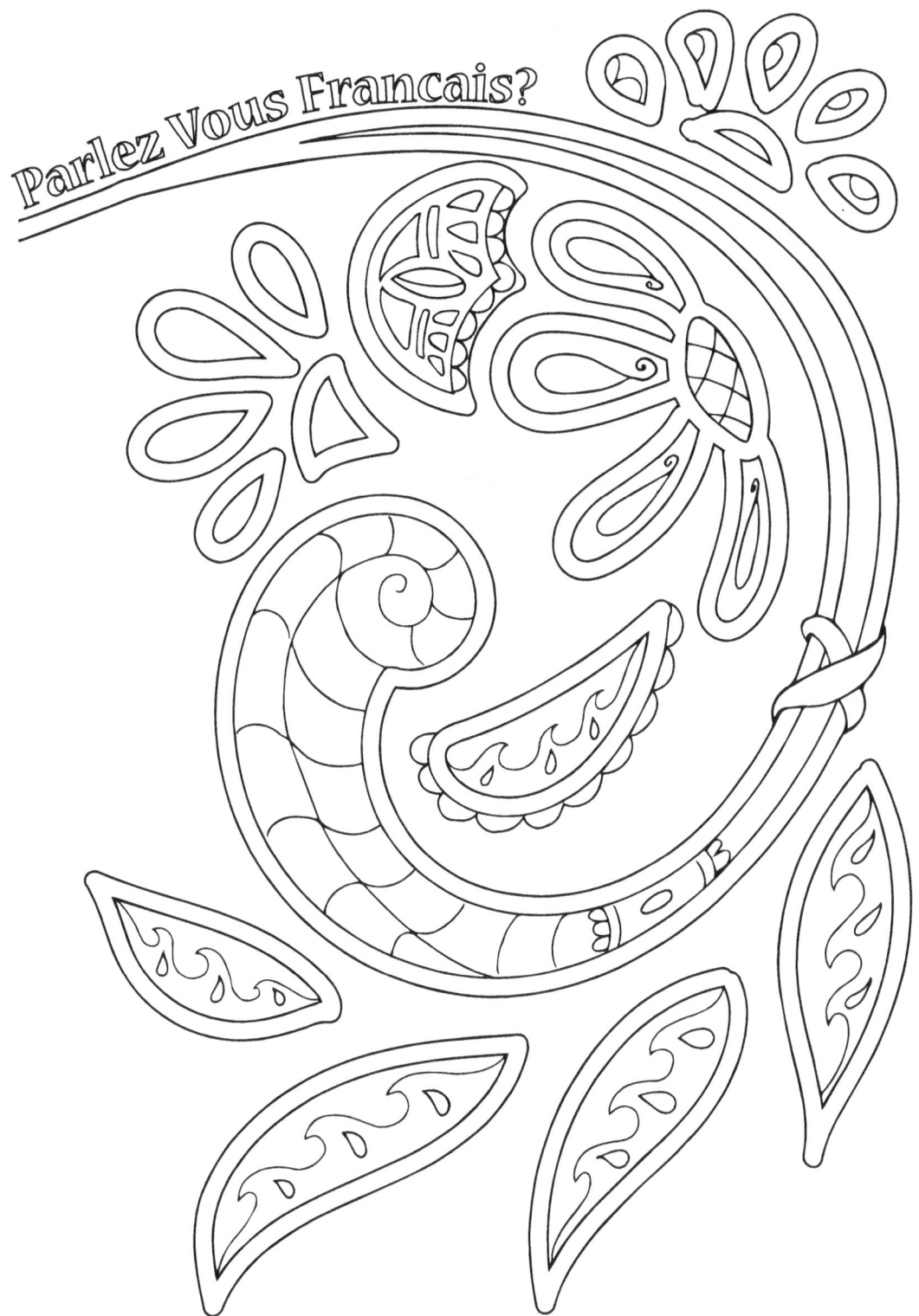

Parlez Vous Francais?

If all else fails...

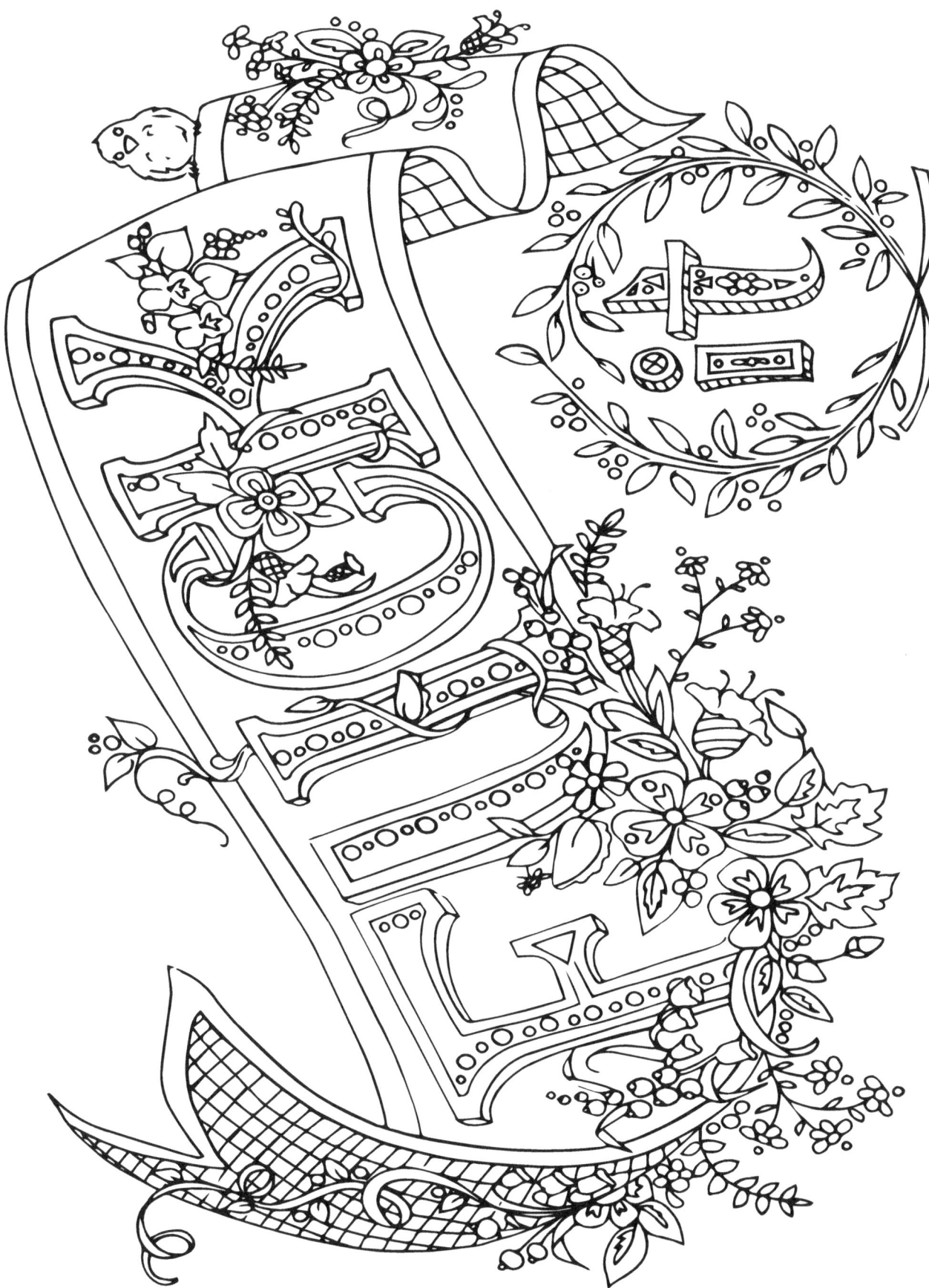

And why do we need to color?

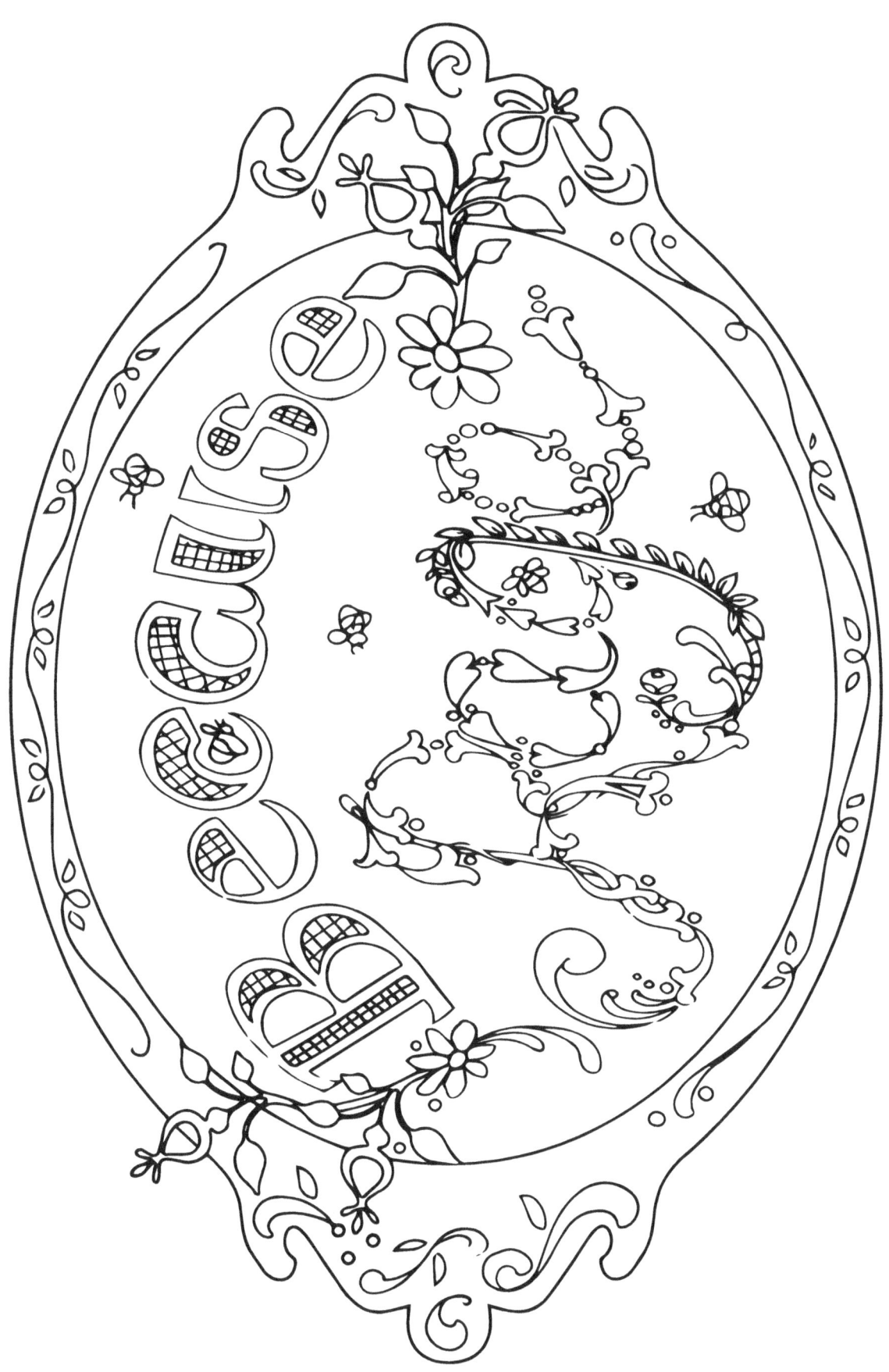

Bye ,Bye now...

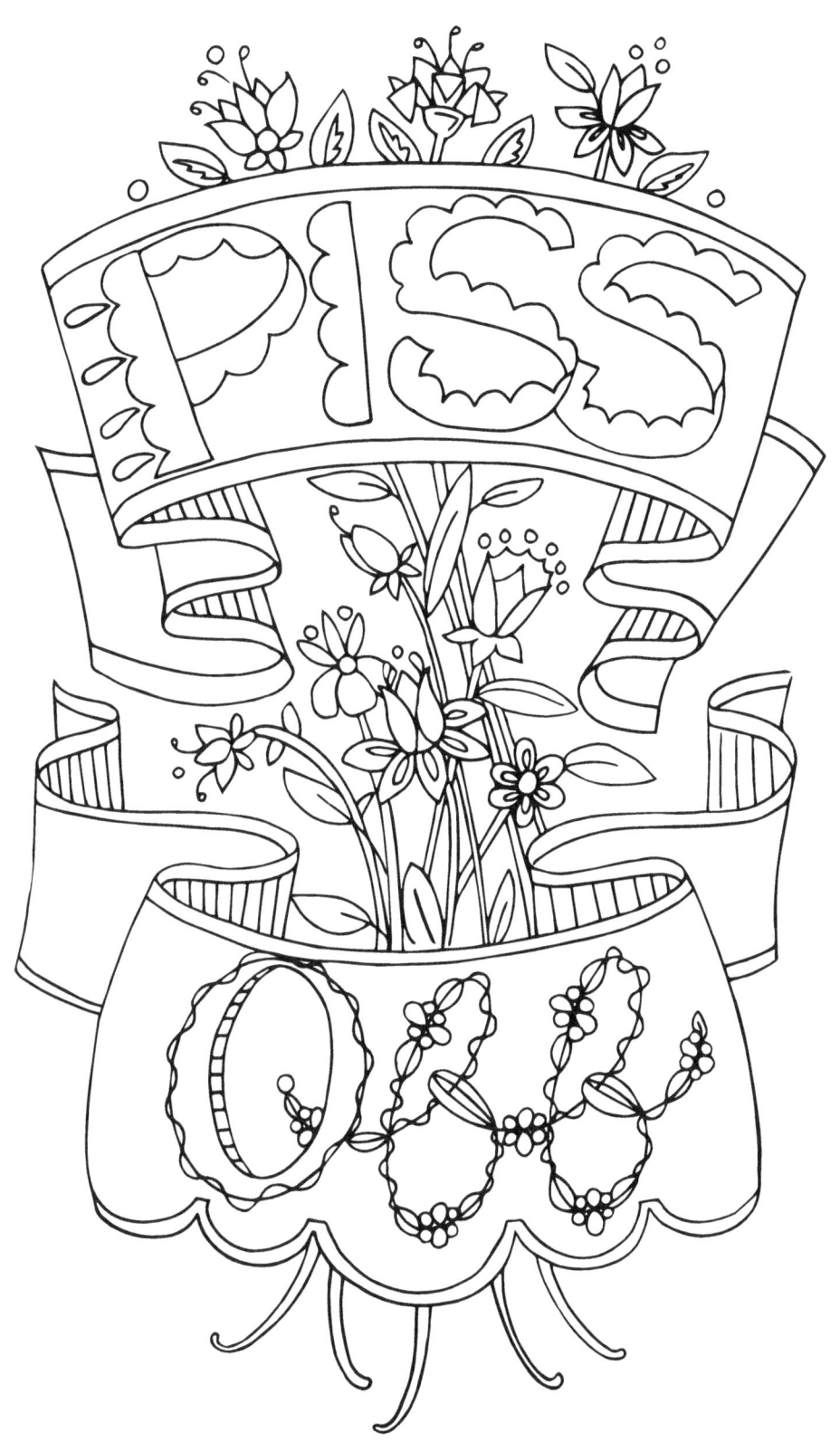

Thanks again for your support!